W9-BXO-193

# THE INVISIBLE CHURCH

## Finding Spirituality Where You Are

*J. Pittman McGehee*
*and Damon J. Thomas*

*Psychology, Religion, and Spirituality*
*J. Harold Ellens, Series Editor*

**Westport, Connecticut**
**London**

**Library of Congress Cataloging-in-Publication Data**

McGehee, J. Pittman.
  The invisible church : finding spirituality where you are / J. Pittman McGehee and Damon J. Thomas.
      p. cm.— (Psychology, religion, and spirituality, ISSN 1546–8070)
  Includes bibliographical references and index.
  ISBN 978–0–313–36530–0 (alk. paper)
  1. Spirituality.  2. Experience (Religion)  3. United States—Church history.
4. Psychology, Religious.  5. Church.  I. Thomas, Damon.  II. Title.
  BV4501.3.M336  2009
  248—dc22      2008037537

British Library Cataloging in Publication Data is available.

Library of Congress Catalog Card Number: 2008037537
ISBN: 978–0–313–36530–0
ISSN: 1546–8070

First published in 2009

Praeger Publishers, 88 Post Road West, Westport, CT 06881
An imprint of Greenwood Publishing Group, Inc.
www.praeger.com

Printed in the United States of America

The paper used in this book complies with the
Permanent Paper Standard issued by the National
Information Standards Organization (Z39.48–1984).

10  9  8  7  6  5  4  3  2  1

*For my family: My best resource for experiencing the transcendent.*
J. Pittman McGehee

*For my parents, Alma Jean and JD Thomas, who gave me enough.*
Damon J. Thomas

# CONTENTS

## Contents

# SERIES FOREWORD

The interface between psychology, religion, and spirituality has been of great interest to scholars for a century. In the last three decades a broad popular appetite has developed for books that make practical sense out of the complicated research on these three subjects. Freud had a negative outlook on the relationship between psychology, religion, and spirituality and thought the interaction between them was destructive. Jung, on the other hand, was quite sure that these three aspects of the human spirit were constructively linked, and one could not be separated from the others. Anton Boisen and Seward Hiltner derived much insight from both Freud and Jung, as well as from Adler and Reik, and fashioned a useful framework for understanding the interface between psychology, religion, spirituality, and human social development.[1] We are in their debt.

This series of General Interest Books, so wisely urged by Praeger Publishers and particularly by its acquisitions editors, Suzanne Staszak-Silva and Debbie Carvalko, intends to define the terms and explore the interface of psychology, religion, and spirituality at the operational level of daily human experience. Each volume of the series identifies, analyzes, describes, and evaluates the issues of both popular and professional interest that deal with the psycho-spiritual factors at play (1) in the way religion takes shape and is expressed, (2) in the way spirituality functions within human persons and shapes both religious formation and religious expression, and (3) in the ways that spirituality is shaped and expressed by religion.

The books in this series are written for the general reader, the local library, and the undergraduate university student. They are also of significant interest to informed professional persons, particularly in fields somewhat related to religion, spirituality, and social psychology. They also have great value for clinical settings, ethical models, and cultural values. I have spent an entire professional lifetime focused specifically upon research into the interface of psychology, sociology, religion, and spirituality. These matters are of the highest urgency in human affairs today when religious motivation seems to be playing an increasing role, constructively and destructively, in the public arenas of social ethics, national politics, and world affairs.

The primary interest in this present volume, *The Invisible Church: Finding Spirituality Where You Are*, by J. Pittman McGehee and Damon J. Thomas, is spiritual, religious, and ethical. In terms of the sciences of theology and religious studies, this volume investigates the operational dynamics of religion and its influence upon notions and experiences of human spirituality, within the socio-historical context of the church's life. The authors address issues that are of universal concern but at the same time very personal and close to home. They have seen through the sham and superficiality of much of the Christian tradition's view of personal spirituality throughout the twenty centuries of the developing church, but particularly in our present day. They also have the objectivity to affirm in ringing terms the heroic strength, insight, honesty, and courage of those sensitive and sensible clerics and laypersons, who have seen through the erroneous and unbiblical attitudes and practices that so often prevail in Christian theology, religious rituals, and biblical ethics.

Puritanism and Evangelical Fundamentalism, in their simplistic beliefs, have excessively influenced American religion and turned it into a pseudo-religion trying to pass itself off as true religion. This is the main force in compelling so many to turn from what they call "organized" religion today. It is not the case that they prefer disorganized religion, of course. They mean, rather, that they find little meaning in the established traditions of *institutionalized* religion as they encounter it in the churches today. Not all of the influences or expression of human spirituality throughout Christian history have been negative or harbored potentially negative consequences. Indeed, much of the impact of the great religions upon human life and culture has been redemptive, and generative of great good, as these authors imply.

It is all the more urgent, therefore, that we discover and understand better what the theological, sociological, and psychological forces are that empower people of faith, moving them to genuine spirituality, giving themselves to all the creative and constructive enterprises that, throughout the centuries, have made of human life the humane, ordered, prosperous, and beautiful experience it can be at its best, in the practice and celebration of spirituality. Spirituality is the irrepressible human quest for personal and communal meaning, mundane (with each other), and transcendent (with God). Surely the forces for good in both religion and spirituality far exceed the powers and proclivities toward the destructiveness and meaninglessness that we too often see in our world today.

Spirituality is the essence of being human. It is the main expression of the inner force of life and personhood. When the central energy of our inherent vitality expresses itself in a transcendent reach for meaning and connection, through our psyches, toward God, we call it transcendent spirituality. When that same force expresses itself horizontally toward another human, we call it love and cherishing ethical relationship. It is the same force. Healthy spirituality is essential to personal wholeness and authentic personhood. That is why it is so urgent that the present disillusion with institutional religion is promptly healed and constructive religion is restored, in service to our hunger for wholesome and genuine spirituality.

McGehee and Thomas demonstrate with numerous detailed illustrations what went wrong with the church's perspective on our spiritual quest and religious practices over the centuries. They suggest, as well, the concrete ways in which this outlook can and must be repaired for humans to enjoy the celebrated and wholesome life that God intended us to experience. This tightly argued, articulate, and highly readable volume is a worthy companion to another recently published Praeger imprint entitled *Understanding Religious Experience: What the Bible Says about Spirituality* (Ellens, 2007).

*J. Harold Ellens*
*Series Editor, Psychology, Religion, and Spirituality*

# PREFACE

I have managed to maintain a foothold in polite company even though I am known to some as a religious liberal, progressive, and even revisionist. Yet my lectures manage to attract a few unsuspecting souls who will audibly gasp when they hear me say that I'm an avowed Marxist-Leninist. While they hear *Marxist-Leninist*, what I'm really saying is *Marxist-Lennonist*—that's Groucho and John, not Karl and Josef. I identify with Groucho because he said he would never belong to any club that would have him as a member, which is the way many of us feel about organized religion, and I love John Lennon because he exhorted us to "Imagine," which is where we ultimately find God and the Divine.

So as a card-carrying Marxist-Lennonist, I offer this book for people who have been wounded by religion. There are so many of us walking wounded out there, particularly in the United States, that one of my greatest anxieties as a young Episcopal priest—the fear of not having enough to keep me busy—never came true. Since I changed my focus and became a depth psychologist in the Jungian tradition, I've been able to build a thriving practice, waiting list and all, around people who have been wounded by religion.

It's nice to be so needed, but if I could somehow by proclamation heal every broken and self-estranged soul out there, I would gladly close up shop and retire to a life of fishing. I have no such illusion about my power to heal anyone, or that the individuation process I want to describe in this book is the answer for everyone. What I do hope is that this discussion will help something to resonate inside of each reader, so that they might begin to find their own path toward the grace, wholeness, and transcendence that true religion offers.

I respect viewpoints like those of the novelist Philip Roth, who has called religion "irrational and delusional," because in its current form, much of it is. But I would argue that we human beings are deeply religious creatures by our very nature. As the religious scholar Karen Armstrong writes, we have evidence that we humans have searched for meaning and value in this often harsh and unfair life ever since we became conscious.

I hope to start a dialogue about what it would take to reclaim our true religious natures, about how we can untangle ourselves from that punitive old-time religion and re-vision a healthy spirituality for the twenty-first century. I believe that the most basic function of religion has to do with making us whole, as suggested by the etymological root of the word. *Legare* means to connect, so *re-legare*, which gives us *religio* and *religion*, is essentially about reconnecting our broken, disconnected, and split-off parts to become whole again. Humpty Dumpty may have been a lost cause, but the healing resources of religion offer us to opportunity to put ourselves back together again.

One of my favorite quotations comes from the Russian playwright and short-story writer Anton Chekhov, who said, "To be conscious without having a philosophy of life is no life at all, but rather a nightmare and a burden."

Having a philosophy, or worldview, helps me find meaning and groundedness in this life. As a Christian, my life has been immeasurably enriched by having access to a sacred story, which for me is all about the power of transformation, renewal, and claiming authority for one's own life. This is not to suggest that Christianity is the only valid worldview, for that would smack of the negative father exclusivity that poisons so much of our religious atmosphere. Yet even a self-described secular humanist such as Kurt Vonnegut has weighed in on the importance of belonging to a larger tribe or family. (Secular humanists have made many great contributions to the world, but as Vonnegut concedes, the tribe is not very organized.)

This is probably the point at which I should disclaim my personal philosophy on religion, sort of like an advisory label on a CD or video game. I consider myself a Christian, and this book is largely about accessing the transformative power of the sacred story and symbols of the Christian myth, but any reader looking for a book that supports a literal view of Christianity or an endorsement of Christianity as the only true religion will probably not find much to agree with in these pages, unless like me they welcome and encourage divergent viewpoints.

And because I am a Jungian analyst, readers will find many references to the psychology of C. G. Jung, the Swiss psychologist who founded the field of analytical psychology in the early twentieth century. Today, many more readers may know about Jung through Dr. Jennifer Melfi, the Jungian analyst played by Lorraine Bracco on *The Sopranos*, than have read his actual writings or those of his primary lay interpreters. But Jung's influence permeates modern psychology more than most people realize. An early protégé of Sigmund Freud, before splitting with him over differences on religion and other issues, Jung originated many concepts that have become commonplace in our psychological vocabulary, including such terms as *complex*, *collective unconscious*, *shadow*, and *anima*.

Jung coined the now ubiquitous term *New Age*, referring not to popular images of chimes and crystals, but to his idea of a fundamental paradigm shift in human consciousness. This shift began to occur around the year 1500, when according to Jung, "God fell out of the heavens and into man's psyche."[1] He also originated the idea that dreams offer us messages from the personal and collective unconscious, speaking to us in a language of universal symbols and archetypes. Perhaps his greatest contribution to humankind was to map out the process of individuation, the lifelong journey we all take toward becoming ourselves and which is central to the Christian myth and this book.

Finally, I want to stress that *myth* is a very substantial word in the Jungian worldview, and far from attempting to trivialize any sacred story, use of the word conveys a deep reverence and recognition for an eternal truth. The best definition of *myth* I've ever heard comes from an apocryphal little boy, who, when asked to define myth, said, "It's something that might not be true on the outside, but it's true on the inside." And that might be where we truly, finally find the elusive kingdom of God—within.

Some might say that I am trying to psychologize religion. Others might view this work as trying to revitalize religion. If I could only make one point about what I believe the Gospel is really about, I believe it means you are free, and that includes the freedom to choose your viewpoint—and your religion.

# Acknowledgments

We would like to acknowledge J. Harold Ellens for finding us. We would like to thank Suzanne Staszak-Silva for representing us. Further, we want to acknowledge Catalina Berg for transcribing hours and hours of courses and lectures in a form that made this book possible. And finally, we want to thank Cathy Trull Jenkins, Pittman's administrative assistant, who manages his professional life, which without her would be unmanageable.

PART I

# Why "That Old-Time Religion" Isn't Good Enough for Anybody

## CHAPTER 1

# THE AMERICAN PSEUDO-RELIGION

I have often preached that if people ever got a whiff of the true Gospel, the churches would soon be empty. For most pew-sitters, the message would seem so scandalous that they would walk out, if not run, as if the buildings were on fire. The few who stayed behind wouldn't remain much longer, for the Gospel they would hear would be so empowering they wouldn't need the church, at least not in its current structure.

My sermonizing includes an intentional dose of hyperbole, but I believe it also carries a substantial grain of truth.

The fact is the churches aren't empty, at least not in America. The United States has the highest rate of church attendance in the developed world, with nearly half of Americans reporting they attend regular church services at least once a week. In Europe, by contrast, these figures range from the high teens to the low single digits.

It is hard to think of another first-world nation with more extraverted religious fervor than the United States, where 90 percent of citizens believe in God, 80 percent identify themselves as Christians, and fully 40 percent are self-professed evangelicals, or born-again Christians.

Despite statistical evidence of an overwhelming Christian majority, I would never support any assertion that the United States is a Christian nation. In our age of increasing religious diversity, such an assertion would be divisive and punitive to those left outside of the chosen circle.

I will state without hesitation that there is a distinct and pervasive American religion, as firmly implanted into our national DNA as Thanksgiving and "The Star-Spangled Banner." Not to be confused with any consciously practiced religion or personal belief system, what I'm calling the American religion is a cultural or ego religion that transcends denomination or creed. In his provocatively titled book, *American Theocracy*, Kevin Phillips calls this same phenomenon our "civil religion."

The American religion is a set of deeply held values, largely unconscious, which has a tremendous influence over our attitudes, both religious and secular. It is the filter through which we form our worldview. Instead of being rose colored, the lens of our national ego religion is red, white, and blue. This may seem sentimentally patriotic, but clear vision it is not.

The main problem with the American religion is that, for a nation where so many millions are so deeply and sincerely religious, the values of our national cultural religion are often at odds with the true Christian values as Jesus taught them. Further, from a mental hygiene point of view, the American religion may actually be unhealthy, both collectively and individually. It is a major reason why, despite our packed megachurches and 24/7 religious broadcasts, America is suffering from a deep spiritual dis-ease, with the evidence stacking up in epidemic levels of violence and diagnosable mental disorders, along with less visible forms of suffering such as chronic anxiety and depression.

Fundamentalist in its simplistic beliefs about the nature of a cause-and-effect and reward-and-punishment universe, the American religion is a pseudo-religion trying to pass itself off as true religion. From our earliest, Puritan beginnings, this religion has always been more about structure and authority than spirituality. Despite popular romantic sentiment, the opposite of love is not hate or indifference, but power. And an obsession with power and control does not bode well for a religion that proclaims love as its highest value.

Because it cuts us off from our own true natures, and prevents us from accessing the deepest meaning of the Gospel, our civil religion carries within it the seeds of self-estrangement and soul sickness. With its rule-centered fixation on reward and punishment, this legalistic religion works to perpetuate its power by keeping people infantilized and dependent, rather than helping them to mature emotionally and become their own authorities.

And being a non-Christian, religious liberal or beloved infidel in this country hardly gets you off the hook. Whether you're a Baptist in the Deep South, a Buddhist in California, a Jew in New York, or a Muslim in Massachusetts, the American religion gets into your bloodstream like malaria. It's passed from generation to generation, through families and institutions. Immigrants also pick it up quickly.

Once in our systems, this religion insidiously promotes the formation of unconscious beliefs and self-judgments about whether we are good or bad, worthy or unworthy—whether we've been productive enough to earn God's grace and abundance, or whether we're doomed to a life of inner and outer impoverishment.

Mark Twain nailed the contagious and pervasive nature of the American civil religion when he said that in religion "people's beliefs and convictions are in almost every case gotten at second hand, and without examination." As I want to lay out, true religion as opposed to pseudo-religion comes from our own inner experience and authority, and examination is mandatory if we are to develop a new liberating form of consciousness. We have no room for anything secondhand or unexamined in our religious lives.

Jungian analyst Murray Stein wrote a book called *Jung's Treatment of Christianity*, which employs the narrative device of casting Jung as the psychoanalyst and Christianity as the patient. It is an excellent book, and I'd like to borrow Stein's analogy and analyze the American religion as the patient on the proverbial couch.

In medicine, diagnosis is the first step to healing, usually followed by drugs or surgery. In psychotherapy, our most powerful resource is consciousness. According to my neurosurgeon friends, conscious people are those who are not asleep or comatose. From a psychological viewpoint, the definition of consciousness is much more complex. It means awareness, self-knowledge, understanding, and the ability to recognize and accept a variety of viewpoints. Consciousness also includes recognizing our dark side, or shadow, where our darkest thoughts and impulses unconsciously reside.

As we delve into analysis, we discover a lot about ourselves along the way. So let us consider what this pseudo-religion means, what it looks and feels like, and how it came to be such a significant part of our individual and collective consciousnesses. Then we will go on to examine how, for so many of us, this religion is the primary contributing factor for the two most powerful and primitive psychological complexes, which together are the root of most psychological suffering.

## OUR PURITAN BLENDER

If Mickey Mouse, Coca-Cola, and MTV are the symbols of the widely recognized American pop culture, then what are the symbols of the largely unconscious American religion? I would argue that its symbols include Santa Claus, the Easter bunny, the gun-toting sheriff of the Wild West, Uncle Sam, and our most sentimental images of God and Jesus—all whipped together in a powerful Puritan Waring blender, an appliance that symbolizes the peculiar American knack for trivializing the sacred and vice versa, getting it all mixed up.

I often tell the story of a Christmas parade I witnessed as a small boy in my hometown of Drumright, Oklahoma. The grand-finale float was a giant birthday cake with tinsel frosting that read, "Happy Birthday, Jesus." As the float reached the end of the parade route, out popped a good citizen in a Santa Claus suit. Talk about blending the sacred and the secular into a mixed metaphor!

Floating around in our American puree, these disembodied sacred and secular symbols such as Jesus and Santa Claus represent the unholy trinity of our civil religion: reward and punishment, cause and effect, and structure over spirituality. One might ask, "Where is God in this American frappe?" "Where is the holiness in this melting pot?" The quick answer is that the American religion has never been much about religion at all, at least not in the truest sense of religion, which is essentially about reconnecting our broken and estranged parts to become whole again.

Although we tend to act as though the American religion is based in scripture, this pseudo-religion is actually only a consensus reality, an outward cultural expression of the American ego. A quick note on the ego is that it is the organ of consciousness, with the primary purpose of ensuring survival. As such, the ego is fraught with anxiety and is staunchly conservative, in the sense of preferring the known over the unknown. In individuals as well as cultures, the ego becomes preoccupied with differentiating between "me and them" and "us and them." It takes false comfort in hubris, gaining a fleeting sense of security by feeling superior, never pausing to consider the obvious truth that a superiority complex is a transparent compensation for an inferiority complex.

Above all, the American religion system seeks to maintain the illusion of fairness, which provides the foundation for a cause-and-effect universe. In a fair world, any action creates a corresponding reaction. If you want to avoid being punished by man or God, then follow the rules. You might even be rewarded. Break the rules and you're certain to suffer the consequences. Even if no external punishment materializes, this highly efficient system ensures suffering through our own self-produced guilt and shame.

The catchall disclaimer to the law of fairness is that if an undeserved misfortune or catastrophe should occur, no matter how inexplicably unfair, it's because "God had a plan." You can hardly argue with God's plan, can you? We immediately judge and neatly dismiss things by saying, "That was horrible!" or "That was a bad thing; it was a sin." Well, that ends that.

We greatly prefer this method to asking more thoughtful and probing questions, such as "Why did this happen?" and "How did I get to this place?" "Where is this leading?" and "How can I be transformed by this?" This is a marvelously effective technique for avoiding the hard work of analysis and the painful process of becoming conscious. The only problem is that the price we pay for remaining unconscious is ultimately much higher.

When "shit happens" and our response is "God had a plan," we never take advantage of the exhilarating opportunity that is always available to us. This is the chance to do what the alchemists could never do: to turn *prima materia* (shit) into gold.

We have wrestled with the dark side of America's Puritan heritage since Nathaniel Hawthorne wrote *The Scarlet Letter* in 1850. As most of us remember from high school or college literature, Hawthorne's masterpiece told the story of Hester Prynne, a married woman who committed adultery in seventeenth-century New England. Prynne was rebuked and forced to forever display her transgression by wearing a scarlet A on her chest. Her "baby's daddy," as we would say today, was none other than the town's highly respected minister, who raises his moral stature by publicly humiliating and interrogating the stoic woman who bore his child but refused to name the father.

From America's politics to its daytime television shows, how many times has a similar scenario of self-righteous hypocrisy played out in the ensuing centuries? Very recently, the *Houston Chronicle* ran a story about an evangelical preacher who was being sued by a member of his church for distributing a letter to the entire congregation, divulging the details of what she assumed was a private marital counseling session. The woman had wanted a divorce, and the preacher urged the congregation to shun her until she saw the error of her ways and recommitted herself to a miserable marriage. Exclusion and punishment, it appears, are very much alive in great swaths of our society.

Lest I seem to be coming down too hard on the United States, let me say that colonial America had nothing on Europe when it came to witch hunts and other forms of religious persecution such as pogroms and inquisitions. But promoting conformity through shaming and exclusion seems to be a particularly homegrown attribute, perhaps because American society was so insular at the time. It was also a largely self-edited population, dominated in its earliest years by zealous Puritans electing to leave the Old World so they could form a New World mirroring their own religious ideals.

Before migrating to America, Puritanism was born into the religious turmoil and upheaval of sixteenth-century Europe, a time when the Western world was undergoing a tremendous, anxiety-producing transformation. It was the beginning of the Enlightenment, or the Age of Reason, and it began the demythologization process that would lead Nietzsche to declare, about three centuries later, that God was dead. We were entering the first time in the Christian era that the entire world, and every aspect of daily life, was not governed by a pervasive mono-myth. New emphasis was placed on *logos*, or man's capacity for reason and rationalism, and mythology was dismissed as irrational.

As the religious scholar Karen Armstrong observes, humankind soon began to suffer at the hands of this "progress":

> As early as the sixteenth century, we see more evidence of a numbing despair, a creeping mental paralysis, and a sense of impotence and rage as the old mythological way of thought crumbled and nothing new appeared to take its place. This alienation was apparent in the reformers who tried to make European religion more streamlined, efficient and modern.[1]

Despair and its cousins exacted a price we are still paying, because as willing or unwitting practitioners of the American religion, we have been unconscious heirs to the ills of our spiritual forefathers.

Martin Luther, John Calvin, St. Augustine, and a fourth-century monk named Pelagius were not Americans, but their theology has had so much influence on the American civil religion (and hence American life) that one could make a strong case for adding them to Mt. Rushmore, or at least someplace in our national landscape. But far from being figures who could be easily Disneyfied for American tastes, each of these religious reformers was ravaged by his own inner demons and complexes, which in turn had a dark influence on his theology.

As Armstrong writes, Martin Luther, the founder of Protestantism, was "prey to agonizing depressions and paroxysms of rage." John Calvin, the father of Puritanism, "shared Luther's utter helplessness before the trials of human existence—a dis-ease that impelled them to find a solution."[2]

Gripped by such stern and stoic demeanors, these men were driven to make religion conform to an orderly and systematic efficiency, with no tolerance for mystery or nonrationality, and very little room for grace. It is no wonder, then, that there is so much truth in the old quip, "Puritanism is the fear that, somewhere out there, somebody is having a good time." You couldn't accuse the Pilgrims of having a good time. Among the earliest new Americans, this separatist group of ultraserious Puritans banished all forms entertainment from their colonies.

The Protestant ethic is the direct descendent of Puritanism, and it has had enormous influence on Western Christianity in general, and on the American religion in particular. Calvin, who loved to use the word *depraved* to describe human beings, was very concerned about the idea of why some people accepted the Christian Gospel while others didn't. He concluded that some people were evidently elected, or predestined, to believe. This doctrine meant that God chose those who would be saved through Christ's sacrifice, for reasons as mysterious as his own nature. Asked how he came to this conclusion, Calvin consulted the Bible and responded with the supporting scripture, "By their fruits you shall know them."

When I was stock boy in a grocery store back in Oklahoma, the fruits (along with the vegetables) were stored in the produce department. That gives us an idea of what "produce" means—the fruits or production of man's hard work on God's earth. So for centuries now, one's production has been seen as the way of proving oneself to be one of the elect or predestined souls who have earned God's favor. The more you produce, the more obvious it becomes that God has blessed you.

In Mormonism, the only completely indigenous American religion, you see the Puritan work ethic in spades. What is polygamy about if not increased production? The beehive, an early Mormon symbol and the official state symbol of Utah, is also about productivity. I'm not saying that production and capitalism are bad. Indeed, there are many positive aspects of these systems. However, I am arguing that we've gotten production mixed up with religion.

This attitude is why one of the highest compliments you can pay an American is to say he or she "has a good work ethic." It's also why the United States lags the rest of the developed world in the time it devotes to leisure and recreation, and our mental, physical, and spiritual fatigue is only getting worse with our newfound addiction to Blackberries, iPods, and other technologies that enable us to be "always on" although "wired and tired." *Crackberry*, a term that neatly sums up the addictive quality of PDAs, has become such a part of the American lexicon that it was selected by *Webster's Dictionary* as the word of the year for 2006.

We're all twenty-first-century coconspirators in this enduring Puritan ethic, no matter how conscious we try to be. I must also plead guilty. A while back, somebody counted up the number of patients that the Swiss-born Jung saw throughout his career, and it was a very low figure. I see more patients in one year than Jung ever saw, and my practice is very slow-paced compared to the 15-minute "med check" appointments that pass for mental health treatment in our country today.

Eastern observers have also commented on the frenzied pace of modern American life as we strive for ever-increasing production, at the same time reflexively avoiding any encounter with consciousness. "We busy ourselves doing as many things as possible, taking refuge in doing more and more, faster and faster. We aren't sleeping well at night and we're not enjoying ourselves during the day," the Dalai Lama said.

The Buddhist monk Thich Nhat Hanh has said that our consumption-based, debt-driven society is home to millions of "hungry ghosts" incapable of finding fulfillment no matter how much is laid out in front of them, for their narrow throats and pinhole mouths could never fill up their huge, distended bellies.

Putting in long hours is one of our highest national values, yet we refuse to do the hard work of becoming conscious, instead preferring to distract ourselves with busy work or numb out with TV. For a nation that promotes religion and hard work as two of its highest values, we may be collectively committing what Jung called the greatest (and I might add laziest) sin of all, which is to remain unconscious.

The Puritan ethic that continues to propel us toward exhaustion was itself strongly influenced by the much older doctrine of Pelagianism, which essentially says that God's love and grace are not free gifts but instead must be earned through work and sacrifice. Pelagius was an ascetic Christian monk born in the British Isles in the fourth century, and his insistence on earned grace, along with his denial of the Augustinian doctrine of original sin, got him branded as a heretic.

Pelagius lost the battle over original sin, which went on to become the cornerstone for the Catholic Church's hopelessly anachronistic teaching that sex is inherently evil, to be tolerated only for procreative purposes. But to our everlasting detriment, he had much greater success in perpetuating his idea about the cost of God's grace—even though it was the exact opposite of what Jesus and Saint Paul taught. Pelagius said free grace was just too scandalous to be true. Even in the fourth century, apparently, there was great suspicion toward the free lunch. No other system provides something for nothing, so why should grace be any different?

Never mind that Jesus, the ultimate Christian authority, taught that grace is available as undeserved favor, a free gift with no strings attached. You don't earn it, you don't even necessarily deserve it—that's the essence of a gift. And as for cause-and-effect or reward-and-punishment, anyone who swears by these systems has not read the wisdom literature nor listened very carefully to what the Rabbi Christ taught.

Jesus says the rain falls on the just and the unjust. He said there is a different kind of economy in the kingdom of God, so that the last are first, the whores are queens and the beggars are kings. And if you work one hour, you get paid the same as those who worked all day. Admittedly, it's a bad economic theorem, but it is the nature of the Gospel as Jesus proclaimed it, regardless of whether Wall Street or Main Street are willing to accept it.

One thing Americans revere almost as much as religion is capitalism, and in many ways capitalism has become an inextricable part of the American religion, with its emphasis on production and prosperity. We have little interest in the nonrational economy that operates in the kingdom of God, and even less in the kingdom's nonmaterial aspects. In our culture, if something is nonrational, it is irrational. If it is nonmaterial, it is immaterial. Words, even particles, matter. *Non* simply implies that something distinct or different; the other particles are loaded with judgment and dismission regarding dimensions of our lives that may be just as valuable—if not more so—than their opposites.

One of the most troubling offshoots of the American religion is the fast-growing prosperity movement, whose followers believe that God wants them to be richly endowed with earthly goods. The values of this movement were summed up by singer Mary J. Blige, who recently said, "My God wants me to bling." Here in Houston, the copastor of one of our largest megachurches has boasted how God granted her wish to live in a fabulously large and opulent home—never mind that Jesus of Nazareth owned nothing more than the garments on his back.

So we have a popular disconnect between the teachings of Christ and this Puritanical viewpoint that's all about proving you are one of the elect, that you have earned God's grace through your demonstrated ability to produce and conform. As popular as it is, this viewpoint is very primitive, in the sense that this is the way children feel about their parents. For many of us who have been under the unconscious influence of the American religion, we have developed an infantile view of God that is essentially a combination of the negative mother and father. As we shall see later, organized religion has willingly exploited and enabled these complexes and this faulty, limited God image as a prime means for keeping people infantilized and dependent, thereby ensuring the survival of the religious organization.

## A SACRED STORY IN A PROFANE STRUCTURE

What I'm working on here is that the religion most of us grew up with, or what most of us understood religion to be, was never religion at all but part of the collective cultural consciousness I'm calling the American religion. It was God contained in a religious structure made up by humans, namely, men.

The theologian Frederick Buechner said that there is a theological church, which is in essence the religion's sacred story about God and his (or her) relationship with humanity. Out of this sacred story comes a set of symbols, traditions, and rituals, such as baptism and the Eucharist in Christianity.

Buechner also said there is the institutional church, which is the structure or organization developed to house the theological church. He envisioned the theological and institutional churches as circles. The optimist, he said, views these circles as concentric, or sharing the same center. The cynic says the circles never touch, that the theological and institutional churches are hopelessly separated. The final view is that of the realist, who says the circles occasionally overlap.

Robert Johnson, who has been a primary translator of Jung's writings for the lay public, has used the image of the mandorla to visualize the relationship between the theological and institutional churches. Not to be confused with the mandala, the mandorla is the holy territory where the circles of sacred story and structure overlap, creating a little slice of wholeness and integration, if only in a limited spectrum of time and space.

I suspect that occasionally there is a church that is the mandorla, or at least a church that is being the mandorla some of the time, but for the most part we have the structure over here, and we have the sacred story over there (if it is present at all). Rarely do the circles of theological and institutional churches come close to touching anymore, because the primary mission of the church has become self-perpetuation, which requires money, power, and a membership that has been made docile and dependent through fear and infantilization.

The problem, therefore, is not so much with the theological church as with the institutional church, which has too often become an amalgamation of many things that don't necessarily have much to do with the sacred story.

What remnants of the sacred story that remain in the institutional church have been so corrupted and perverted through the centuries that they have lost their energy and transformative power. For myself and a growing number of twenty-first century seekers, true religion is increasingly found in what I call the "invisible" church. As unseen yet also as real as the spirit or soul, the invisible church is substantive enough to contain the sacred stories and symbols of Christianity or any other faith tradition. Freed from the corruptive influence of the institutional church, the invisible church can offer enough structure and tradition to allow its "members" to benefit from millennia of collective imaginings of the relationship between the divine and the human, while providing the freedom for each to individuate and claim his or her own authority.

In our American experience, the singular purpose of our ego religion has been to civilize and provide structure to a wild, virginal continent—which by the way was a near-perfect metaphor for the feminine archetype that had been so devalued by Western religion. Nature is archetypally feminine, and the Native Americans, with their instinctuality and reverent attitude toward Mother Earth, were in many ways a feminine society. The colonists brought with them a very patriarchal structure that had been honed for millennia, and they got right to work imposing their masculine God image and Puritan worldview on this untamed land.

"Cultures take purposes for themselves, cling tenaciously to them, and exalt them into the purposes and meaning of life itself," wrote the late, great social critic Jane Jacobs. In the formative years of the American nation, she wrote, "the purpose of life became the salvation of souls, one's own and others."[3]

From the first settlements on the eastern seaboard to the relentless drive westward, the American myth has been all about civilizing a wild continent and replacing chaos with law and order, both civilly and religiously. That's how the Old West sheriff got into our Puritan blender and why there's no female equivalent of Uncle Sam. It's also why the American psyche is so dependent on rules and structure.

I am not against structure or civilization. Our human need for structure is so fundamental and archetypal that if we did away with all the structures today, they would reappear within the next generation. And the rules and structures that have been passed down to us are very useful, a transpersonal heritage that has served humankind fairly well throughout history, sparing us from having to reinvent the wheel in every generation.

We get into trouble when we become overly obsessed with rules, when we become rule centered and legalistic, and this is the nature of American religion. So much of what we grew up with was espoused by a patriarchal, hierarchal structure that not only included our churches, but also our schools, families, and governments. The message we got from all these influential institutions was that we lived in a cause-and-effect universe governed by a system of rewards and punishments for our behavior.

It's not uncommon in American life to hear the exasperated refrain, "We worked hard, played by the rules, and then _____"—something bad happened. If you work hard and play by the rules, you certainly don't deserve to see your pension or health-care plan evaporate before your very eyes, as has become so common in the United States. That is a fair expectation, but we also have the idea that a "work hard and follow the rules" contract also applies to a stern parental figure in the sky.

Most of us grew up thinking that if we had a bad thought, or behaved in a way that was contrary to the normative adaptive and conforming behavior, we would be immediately punished. This was among our earliest, most formative ideas about religion. Even when we were not in church and directly mindful of God, his stand-in was our no-nonsense teacher, police officer, or parent. I grew up thinking that the paradigm of the American male was J. Edgar Hoover. He was a man's man, right? As head of the FBI, he not only enforced the codes and punished the rule breakers, but did so with tremendous zeal. We've since found out that the cross-dressing Hoover wasn't the he-man he pretended to be. He was the opposite, which is so often the case with those who are so far to one extreme.

I came of age when polio was an omnipresent fear in American society, much greater than our recent anxiety over AIDS because you could actually catch polio by just going outside, and the disease had no cure or even passable treatment before Salk's vaccine. All the authority figures told us to avoid public places, take a bath every day, and wash our hands after going to the bathroom. That was all sound and loving advice, but the fearful atmosphere was so generalized that I vividly remember my own great fear: that if I didn't wash my hands, I would contract polio by the time I got to the hallway.

Such irrational, generalized fear is normal for children, who haven't yet developed the resources to become their own authorities. Yet even as adults, most of us still carry around this primitive and immature attitude about religion, the penultimate system of reward and punishment. Our waking moments, and even our dreams, are constantly governed by that inner voice that judges us as "good girl" or "bad boy." Our core belief is that if we don't follow the rules to the letter of the law, we will be punished, shamed, or excluded. Or all of the above.

One of my earliest indoctrinations into the American religion came through my Sunday school teacher in Drumright. I imagine that she was perfectly representative of her genre in small-town America, the polar opposite of a sophisticated, educated, and conscious religious authority. The wife of the principal of schools in our town, she pretty much espoused her husband's philosophy of running a well-ordered classroom. This, of course, was that if you behaved you would be rewarded, which frequently equated to just not being punished. And if you did misbehave, punishment was certain, whether it was the paddle, a bad report, or a withering look.

Central to our rule-fixated culture is this illusion and lie that says following the rules constitutes moral behavior. Following the rules does not make you moral or ethical. It makes you highly adapted and conformed, out of the ego's fear of punishment. Following the rules is legalism, not morality. Indeed, to be truly moral, you often have to break the rules.

This is about the point where, when I'm giving a lecture, I can see at least one person beginning to think that I'm promoting anarchy. Let me be very clear that I am not. I'm mostly in favor of rules, and I break very few. What I am promoting is autonomy, which is far different from anarchy, because if I am autonomous, than means I will take individual responsibility for my life, my decisions and actions. If I am going to break a rule, I am going to be conscious of what I'm doing, and I am going to do it only for a higher purpose. Otherwise, I'm not being autonomous, but sociopathic.

Many times, the rules we are asked to follow are unhealthy for us as individuals, and we need to be careful about unconsciously accepting rules that feel contrary to our true selves. Despite the sanction and authority given to rules by powerful structures such as the church or government, they sometimes represent the dark side of the code-setting father archetype. When we make the difficult decision to reject an unhealthy rule, we begin to grow up and claim our own authority, and we begin building our own souls. As important as it is, this process is seldom easy or without risk, for we are saying no to some very powerful authoritarian structures.

Thankfully, we have some inspiring role models for breaking the rules, including the radical founder of Christianity. Jesus was very clear that the law was made for us, and that we weren't made for the law, as he expounded to those who criticized him for healing the sick on the Sabbath, the day of rest.

Also, consider Rosa Parks or any protester who has broken any unfair, punitive, and anachronistic law in pursuit of justice. Parks' obligation to give up her seat to a white person was not just a tradition, but a law, backed by the full faith of some powerful local, state, and national governments, not to mention an oppressive culture that was lynching African Americans left and right. But Parks broke that rule and launched the civil rights movement in the process. Prior to that, African Americans in Montgomery, Alabama, and everywhere else in the United States largely adhered to laws that were not only unhealthy but downright savage and inhumane. Was adherence to those laws morality, or conformity out of fear of punishment? And when Parks made her heroic decision to keep her seat, was that immoral?

In the movie, *Cider House Rules*, based on the John Irving novel, the patriarch of the itinerant farm-working clan had little patience when the newcomer Homer, the only literate one among them, started to read off the rules of conduct that had been written on the wall long ago. "They ain't our rules,

Homer. Someone who don't live here made those rules," the old man said. "We didn't write them; I don't see no need to read them." Sometimes you got to break some rules to set things straight, he added, a statement Jesus would have approved of.

Following Jesus' example, it seems to me that becoming conscious and becoming our own authorities is the most moral act of all. It also seems that promoting autonomy would be a natural value of the religion and the church, but that has not happened and shows no sign of happening.

## WHERE IS THE LIVING WATER?

Our cultural religion may not be the religion that churches should be propagating, especially if a church aspires to be a mandorla. William Willimon, a professor of divinity at Duke University, said that Christianity lost its vitality when it came up out of the catacombs and ceased to be countercultural. John Spong, the former Episcopal bishop of Newark, pinpoints the loss of Christianity's true message at a slightly later date, when the Roman Emperor Constantine gave the religion its social and political legitimacy early in the fourth century.

If the church—or *a* church—began to propagate a religion that was in some important ways counter to the dominant, pervasive cultural religion, perhaps we could revitalize Christianity as a force for wholeness and healing. For starters, such a church would offer a vision of the kingdom of God as a place where the nonrational and nonmaterial are at least as valuable as their counterparts, and it would preach the transformative, resurrectional grace of Jesus Christ as a symbol of the Self.

Like so many other institutions, churches don't do a very good job of preserving their original energy and mission statement as they grow. When you begin to form a community around a life-changing and transforming experience, the first thing people want to do is share that experience with others. You need some structure to do that, and before you know it, a living reality becomes a dead tradition.

Ted Waddell, who was head of an Episcopal organization called The College of Preachers, was fond of telling a parable set on the harsh New England coast, in a particular area where the winds, tides, and rocks made for treacherous conditions. There were many shipwrecks, and as the carnage mounted, some very well-meaning and altruistic people decided that they were going to set up a rescue station right at that spot, so that when there were big shipwrecks or small boat wrecks, they would be there to take the wounded and the dying into their warm, dry structure and provide healing for them.

It got to be such an important and well-known rescue station that people from all over came to volunteer there. And as the community centered around the rescue station grew, they had to build a bigger place to house the volunteers and the people who came to witness these charitable acts of healing. Soon the people who built the new clubhouse were arguing about whether they should allow the wet, bleeding, and dying people to come inside anymore.

So they built a rough structure out back for the people from the shipwrecks, so that they wouldn't have to come in and mess up the beautiful new clubhouse. And as the years went on, the club grew and everyone got together on a regular basis and told the story of how they used to rescue people. But nobody got rescued anymore.

Johnson recounts what is basically the same parable in another form, noting that it was said to be Jung's favorite story:

> The water of life, wishing to make itself known on the face of the earth, bubbled up in an artesian well and flowed without effort or limit. People came to drink of the magic water and were nourished by it, since it was so clean and pure and invigorating. But humankind was not content to leave things in this Edenic state. Gradually they began to fence the well, charge admission, claim ownership of the property around it, make elaborate laws as to who could come to the well, put locks on the gates. Soon the well was the property of the powerful and the elite. The water was angry and offended; it stopped flowing and began to bubble up in another place. The people who owned the property around the first well were so engrossed in their power systems and ownership that they did not notice that the water had vanished. They continued selling the nonexistent water, and few people noticed that the true power was gone.[4]

These stories tell what happens when institutions lose the living water that originally brought them into being, informing us that we must drink from the water or it will cease to flow. The water doesn't dry up, but instead reappears in a new place, giving us another chance to drink its life-giving essence. A big question right now is, "If the living water has dried up in the old structures, where can we find it today?" Jesus made the same point when he said that old wineskins won't hold new wine, so where can we find new wineskins?

Many people have a deep longing to find a church or religion that is the mandorla, a church with enough structure to function as an organization, but one that also keeps the sacred story alive and keeps the mystery present. For many, the search has been so wounding and disappointing they given up on religion altogether, hence the popular expression, "I'm not religious, I'm spiritual."

I understand where "I'm not religious, I'm spiritual" comes from, but I don't believe it offers us enough sustenance for our spiritual journey. We humans are deeply religious beings by our very natures, each of us possessing an archetypal urge for an inner life that is rich with myth, symbolism, and mystery. So there is an urgent need for us to reclaim our religious nature, no matter how badly we have been damaged by organized religion. Ironically, the best healing for a bad religious experience is a good religious experience. It's part of the homeopathic law of nature: like heals like.

But in a culture so predominantly committed to remaining unconscious, many Americans have turned to megachurches, most of which are little more than contemporary entertainment centers. It appears that, as a nation, we've chosen entertainment over enlightenment. We've stopped drinking the living water of Christianity, and the truth has dried up, leaving us with so many preachers shouting louder and louder, hoping deaf people will hear.

Even worse, many people are getting caught up in the rising tide of fundamentalism that continues to wash across America. Fundamentalism is the American cultural religion on steroids, with a militant, authoritarian, and exclusionary theology that insists on a literal, concretized doctrine. Why would so many people buy into a rigid, dominating viewpoint that is hellbent on viewing humans as miserable, unworthy sinners? Why would anyone surrender their soul to a dry, brittle theology that is actually unhealthy and harmful, not to mention dead? In a word, it's mostly about anxiety.

## CHAPTER 2

# THE RISING TIDE OF ANXIETY AND FUNDAMENTALISM

The greatest problem in the world today is religion—the kind of fundamentalist religion that takes advantage of unconscious people by exploiting their fears and threatening punishment and exclusion, regardless of what part of the world it occurs in.

I don't generally agree with writers such as Sam Harris, who had two huge best-sellers in 2006, including *The End of Faith*, which basically argues that religion is a collective delusion. While I agree with some of his points, I believe this kind of wholesale dismissal of religion is a part of the "throwing the baby out with the bathwater" syndrome I will discuss later, which errs in denying the undeniably religious nature of the human psyche. But I do think that Harris got right to the heart of the type of zealotry that only religion seems to be able to inspire:

> Religion raises the stakes of human conflict much higher than tribalism, racism or politics ever can, as it is the only form of in-group/out-group thinking that casts the differences between people in terms of eternal rewards and punishments.[1]

And, I might add, religion is the only system that purports to offer divine rewards to believers for acting as agents of "God's will," meting out punishments ranging from exclusion to genocide for nonbelievers. Tolerance for different viewpoints is a proud part of the liberal religious tradition, but perhaps the time has come for us to exercise the father archetype's function of setting limits and boundaries. This function is necessary for the survival of a society and can be helpful, however wary we must be of its dark side.

So a positive, healthy patriarchal voice would say today, "No, you can't do that. The type of fundamentalism that hurts, excludes, and punishes people is wrong. It is spiritual violence, and it has no place in our society."

For the record, I've taken my share of shots from fundamentalists in my 25 years of speaking publicly about religion. Fundamentalists think I'm the Antichrist, while on the other hand, rationalists think I'm a hopeless navel gazer. I find it very validating to be criticized by both sides! This is the first time I've taken such a strong stance against fundamentalism, but I believe the times call for someone to speak out.

There has been a flurry of books documenting the rise of fundamentalism in American religion. Jimmy Carter's take on the situation, *Our Endangered Values*, spent a long time on the best-seller list. In one anecdote, Carter recounts how he welcomed the new president of the Southern Baptist Convention, the nation's largest religious denomination, for a routine White House ceremony in 1979, a few weeks before the Iranian hostage crisis began. They had what Carter thought was a brief and pleasant meeting, until the Baptist leader turned to him upon leaving and said, "We are praying, Mr. President, that you will abandon secular humanism as your religion." In his book, Carter recalls feeling shocked: "I considered myself to be a loyal and traditional Baptist, and had no idea what he meant."[2]

It didn't take long before we all figured out what he meant, for the emergence of the Moral Majority that vaulted Ronald Reagan into power was about to begin its long ascendancy. I agree with that 1980s bumper sticker, "The Moral Majority Is Neither," but this vocal minority quickly succeeded in moving the concept of what constitutes acceptable religious doctrine so far to the right that even a traditional Christian such as Jimmy Carter found himself excluded.

Carter writes that he had at heart always considered himself a fundamentalist, someone inclined to "cling to unchanging principles." But even he couldn't measure up to the standards of the new fundamentalism, which insists on theological rigidity, an authoritarian male leadership determined to dominate women and fellow believers, and an exclusionary us-versus-them worldview.

Proclaiming absolute truth and demanding blind obedience lead the list of five warning signs for "when religion becomes evil," according to a book of the same title by Charles Kimball, a professor of religion and ordained Baptist minister. (In case you're curious, the other three signs include establishing an "ideal" time for when God will reign, claiming that the end justifies the means, and declaring holy war. Fundamentalism seems to fit all or most of these criteria, does it not?)

Why does fundamentalism have such a strong grip on the American psyche as we enter the twenty-first century, with all it promises of unprecedented freedom and progress? My colleague Jim Hollis, a prolific author and director of the Jung Center in Houston, describes fundamentalism as an explicit rejection of modernity and pluralism:

> What might be embraced as the greatest freedom to choose in human his-
> tory instead stirs anxiety in many. Fundamentalism, be it religious or po-
> litical or psychological, is an anxiety management technique that finesses
> the nuances of doubt and ambiguity through rigid and simplistic belief
> systems. If I can persuade myself that the world is perpetually founded on
> the values of another, culturally limited, less conscious age, then I do not
> have to address the new subtleties of moral choice, the emergent capacities
> of women, the ambiguities of gender, sexual identity, and preference, and
> the horrors of nationalism, factionalism, and other tribal mentalities.[3]

Fundamentalism is a territorial, reptilian attitude rooted in the negative side of the father archetype. If you want to establish your authoritarian
worldview, the first thing you do is claim that your religion has the only
truth, delivered direct from God to you or your chosen prophet. This type of
exhaustive, final revelation is very appealing to those who are anxious about
how to live their lives and who are seeking clear, concrete answers to eternal
questions such as, "Where am I going?" and "What is this all about?"

The fundamentalist claim is that we have the answers to those universal
questions and our answers are not only the truth, but the only truth. If you
are inside this circle, you have truth and therefore salvation. If you're outside,
you don't. And that's all there is to it. It couldn't be more simple or black
and white.

So we have some self-elected prophets who not only understand God, but
to whom God speaks and tells how I should live my life. I agree with my fellow Oklahoman Will Rogers, who said, "It ain't them that don't know that
bother me. It's them that think they do, and don't."

I believe that the ultimate questions in life are just that. There is tremendous spiritual value to be found in discussing and living these questions, but
I don't think they have final answers, at least not that we can uncover with
our limited human consciousness. If we try to fix or concretize the answers,
we end up trivializing these ultimate questions.


## THE ROOTS OF FUNDAMENTALISM

A fairly recent phenomenon in the historical context, fundamentalism
grew out of American Protestantism in the 1920s, when a sizable minority of
theologians and their followers began to feel alienated and embattled in an increasingly modern society. If the seventeenth-century Age of Reason chipped
away at the fortified castle of Christianity, then the twentieth century delivered the equivalent of a series of sustained nuclear blasts.

Though Darwin's theory of evolution had been around since 1859, the real showdown came in 1925 with the Scopes Monkey Trial, which eventually led to the teaching of evolution instead of creationism in public schools. The century also brought godless communism and socialism; the Holocaust; the cold war; the Beat generation and the counterculture; the ban on public school prayer; the civil rights, women's rights, abortion rights, and gay rights movements; and lastly, the Internet age of global outsourcing, chronic layoffs, and online predators. All this while the familial, geographic, and economic structures of American society underwent rapid transformation. People became increasingly dispersed and rootless, to the point where some have questioned the value of traditional cemeteries, since so few live near their place of origin. Long-standing social contracts on job security, health care, and education fell by the wayside, leaving huge segments of the population to fend for themselves.

Is it any wonder we're so anxious? Anxiety has been called America's No. 1 mental health problem, with over 18 percent of the U.S. adult population (or 40 million souls) affected by anxiety disorders, according to Anxiety Disorders Association of America. Note that this statistic just covers anxiety disorders, which are serious mental illnesses with strict guidelines for diagnosis. We don't have any reliable numbers on how many Americans suffer from anxiety, but my opinion is that the number, if it were known, would be staggering.

It is normal for us to feel some anxiety, for anxiety is a survival resource, and we would not have made it as a species without it. We go about our daily lives with a normal existential level of anxiety that ranks around 3 on a scale of 1–10, and this level can go up or down temporarily, depending on the circumstances. It's when the level gets up to about 5 and stays there that we begin to become dysfunctional.

There are piles of anecdotal evidence, and plenty of gut testimonials, about how much we suffer beyond an acceptable level of anxiety. Consider this summation, published in *USA Weekend,* from Harvard Medical School epidemiologist Ronald Kessler, who coauthored a World Health Organization study on anxiety:

> A lot of it has to do with the world in which we live. It's a scary place and time. People are moving to strange cities, taking jobs in new industries; there's a lot of uncertainty about the future. Bad things that happen to people are on the rise. Look at the evening news: murders, car accidents, terrorist bombs. This stuff is out there in the popular imagination and making us worried.[4]

Sounds like a snapshot of the American mood on September 12, 2001, doesn't it? It was actually written a year earlier, which just goes to show that anxiety has been with us for a long time, and it's doing nothing but getting worse now that we live in a post-9/11 world where our illusion that our borders and oceans would keep the rest of the world at bay has been shattered.

It is hardly surprising that the simplicity and certainty of a bygone era—the first century—looks so appealing to an awful lot of people, to the point where almost half of the American population identifies itself as fundamentalist, or evangelical. Many more people cling to religious structures that are at least very rigid, if not fundamentalist.

Some psychologists have gone so far as to describe fundamentalism as a psychosis or mental illness, and there are certain cases where this would be an accurate diagnosis. It's not my intent to be divisive or to ridicule deeply held beliefs, but let's take the stance that a fundamentalist worldview is indicative of a pervasive sense of dis-ease about the world and one's place in it. It's not just that fundamentalism is not my style. As a healer, I'm quite convinced that fundamentalism is harmful to the human spirit, and in a very insidious manner.

There is an old saying that if you see someone pointing to the moon, look at the moon, not the finger. Fundamentalism makes people afraid to look past the finger, with the tragic result that its followers never experience the wondrous and transformative Gospel of Christianity. Quite possibly, too, they miss out on their very lives.

## THE FEARFUL EGO

In his book *Denial of Death*, Ernst Becker says the total motivating factor of all religion is fear of death. This truth has been echoed throughout history by sages including the Greek philosopher Epicurus, who wrote: "It is possible to provide security against other ills, but as far as death is concerned, we men live in a city without walls." More recently, the novelist Philip Roth offered this equation of death in a National Public Radio interview: "Think of all the things you feared in life and add them up, and now multiply it by 1,000, and (that's what) you're confronting."[5]

Survival is the ego's strongest instinct, and its greatest fear is that of nonbeing. It's been that way ever since mankind became conscious of what the early twentieth-century Baptist preacher Carlyle Marney called "the canker in the bowel of humanity," otherwise known as death. The Neanderthal cave paintings reveal mankind's earliest known effort to create a counternarrative that would offer some hope of life after death. We know we are here with a birth we didn't request and a grave we can't escape, so what are we to do in the meantime but worry and feel anxious?

I'm fond of saying that in spite of what many people seek from religion, which is life after death, for me Christianity is about life after birth, which is the only life I know. If prevention of death is religion's function, then it has not yet had one success, including the founder of Christianity.

The ego's anxious nature is very conducive to fundamentalism, or at least a highly structured and rigid form of religion. The minute the ego clears the birth canal, the first questions it asks are, "Who's in charge here? How do I survive? Somebody please tell me the rules so I can make it." This is where religion gladly exploits our most primal and fundamental fear, ushering itself in to promise that we can escape death and punishment if we will just follow the rules.

The ego wants and needs a structured religion. A friend who taught me to bass fish said, "The fish are where the structure is." So if there is a sunken tree, dock, or rock, that's where the fish tend to go. That's where they feel safe, and we're no different. There is security in structure, particularly when we are young. Children need authority, and the child in all of us wants somebody to stand up and say, "These are the rules, and if you break them you get your butt kicked, or kicked out."

The rigid structures that are appropriate for children are limiting and dysfunctional for adults. It's understandable that the structures are there to help us through the anxiety, but too many of us get stuck in these early developmental stages in our religious lives. Most of us will abdicate to an authority or a structure because we're so anxious and we want to know what the truth is, rather than discern it for ourselves and become our own authorities.

The entire history of the evolution of human consciousness has been around the issue of authority, and the opening that our natural anxiety provides for authority figures and structures to creep into our consciousness and take advantage. This evolution has been a very dramatic and laborious process, and along the way, the ego has not been a friend to the kingdom of God. With its single-minded focus on survival and prosperity, the ego has not been much interested in things that are nonrational and nonmaterial, and it is not very good at consciously holding paradoxes, those life-affirming, soul-building opportunities to recognize that two things can be true at once.

At this point in time, we must conclude that, based on our experience and evidence, the ego has not evolved very far. All we have to do is look around ourselves to see humans primarily involved with surviving in the outer world and constantly engaged in primitive, reptilian struggles over geographic and ideological territories.

True religion encourages people to throw away the structures and learn to become their own authorities, which despite its promise of freedom is a serious and sobering responsibility. True religion teaches us how to live in the midst of the anxiety, because that's where the growth is. There's such a thing as divine anxiety, which I'll discuss later, and that is what leads to transformation. On a secular level, our society is enamored with the attitude that urges us to work through our fears and "Just do it," but we have not applied that credo to our spiritual lives.

## DOES GOD REALLY HAVE A PLAN?

We want so badly to believe we can predict how the world's going to be that we create illusions such as fairness, a widespread ego defense against the anxiety created by the chaotic, unpredictable, and capricious nature of life. We want to believe in fairness despite the fact that we've all grown up with a grandmother who said, "Life's not fair." Jesus of Nazareth also said life wasn't fair. If it was, Pontius Pilate would've died on the cross, and Jesus would've died in his bed.

There is no myth, sacred story, or even any novel that has fairness as its theme. As Jesus said, "The rain falls on the just and unjust," which is hardly a fair system. But despite all empirical evidence to the contrary, our desire to believe in the illusion of fairness is so strong that it makes us vulnerable to a religious structure that promises us with all certainty, "If you do this, then this will happen. If you do that, then that will happen. Follow the rules, and you'll be rewarded. Break the rules, and you'll be punished."

When something bad happens, the common response is, "God had a plan," because that protects the ego against the terrifying thought of random chaos. If God had a plan, that explains it! Visibly relieved, we exclaim, "No wonder!" The only trouble is that religion with no wonder is hardly religion at all. In removing all the doubt and ambiguity from life and religion, we throw the baby out with the bathwater, leaving no room for wonder, mystery, and novelty. What's left is only a dry, brittle theology, which is why I believe that anxiety is the greatest enemy of true religion.

The truth is that God doesn't have a plan, and we are truly on our own. You can look at this from one viewpoint and conclude that this life then offers an incredibly exhilarating opportunity to make our own journey and become our own authority, but most people won't or can't accept that idea. We can hardly blame the poor ego. Anxiety hurts, and the emotional pain can be overwhelming at times. So here comes fundamentalism with its beguiling promise, "We will soothe your anxiety by giving you rules, boundaries and limits. All you have to do is to abdicate your internal authority to our structure, and we'll make all those hard decisions for you."

Anxiety isn't the only state of being that produces the need for unpleasant decisions the ego would rather not make. The ego has a similar distaste for ambiguity, which means that something may be vague, uncertain, or have two or more possible meanings. Nor does it like ambivalence, which is to say that there are two valences here, and I could go with either. So the ego feels threatened by all these A words—*anxiety*, *ambiguity*, and *ambivalence*—and it is all too glad to abdicate the painful, messy process of decision making.

It's worth noting that *de-cide* comes from the same root as *homi-cide* and *sui-cide*. This makes is clear to see that when you make a decision, you are choosing for something to live and for another thing to die.

With so many choices and decisions to make, we are faced with saying no to another and yes to ourselves, or saying no to ourselves and yes to another. Choices can be hard, and we don't like facing that homicide-suicide dilemma. Through the centuries, there has never been a shortage of people and institutions who, in their own neurotic states of narcissism and inflation, have been only too happy make our decisions for us.

This may take away our anxiety, but it also robs us of our authority, and that is hardly a fair trade. Because if we never decide, we never really live. Every decision is death dealing and life giving, and ability to decide is this grace and burden of being human.

One of the things I would like to avoid is getting into an elitist conversation of us-versus-them. We all have a certain fundamentalist character. I am no exception, and in my own analysis, I realized that part of my motivation for going into the priesthood was to ease my anxiety. There are times I would love to have something for once in my life that is absolutely true and concrete, just the way the Bible says it. Another part of me would like to agree with the evolutionary psychologists and say, "You know, religion really is just a fabrication we came up with to help us feel better."

I have both a fundamentalist and a skeptic in me, and I understand those two extremes because they are part of me. If we're going to be good twenty-first-century theologians, however, we must not allow ourselves to be seduced by either extreme, as difficult as it is to live in between.

It is important to remember that the fundamentalist mind-set is not necessarily limited to religion. There are scientific fundamentalists, and there are even Jungian fundamentalists who quote *The Collected Works* of Jung as if they were holy scriptures.

The National Academy of Science recently created a controversy when the Dalai Lama was invited to speak at one of its gatherings. Some fundamentalist scientists within the academy objected strenuously, claiming that the Dalai Lama's message about enlightenment, mystery, and all that stuff was antithetical to hard science. How close minded! Similarly, when the Dalai Lama also spoke to the Academy for Neuroscience in 2005, some protestors said that if he was not presenting hard data, he should not be allowed to speak.

The Dalai Lama then exhibited a moral courage that should serve as an example to scientific and religious fundamentalists alike. He said, "If science proves some belief of Buddhism wrong, then Buddhism will have to change. In my view, science and Buddhism share a search for the truth and for understanding reality. By learning from science about aspects of reality where its understanding may be more advanced, I believe that Buddhism enriches its own worldview."

To which I can only add, "Amen." What a contrast the Dalai Lama presents to the so-called religious leaders who run about making irresponsible statements about God's will and the punishment implicit in natural and man-made disasters ranging from hurricanes to the September 11 attacks.

## THE MOST HERETICAL THEOLOGY

Exploiting anxiety is not the only strategy fundamentalism has used to keep so many people infantilized and dependent. Another method has been to claim that this life is just the preparation for another, eternal life. The promise is that if you surrender your authority and follow the rules during this earthly life, you'll be rewarded with a new, everlasting life with none of the anxiety or other problems that plague our worldly existence. Of all the theological theories I know of, I see this one as the most heretical.

According to the wisdom and the traditions I trust, and according to the worldview and authority I've worked so hard to develop for myself, the kingdom of heaven is not something we're aspiring to later. It is something that is available to us in the here and now, and we know this kingdom is archetypal—an eternal transpersonal truth valid in all times and places—because Jesus was not the only prophet to talk about it. This is the point where many fundamentalists get outraged and nervous, because this challenges their claim of possessing the only truth. On the other hand, I find the archetypal universality of the idea of the kingdom of heaven to be very affirming and liberating.

I have often sermonized that Jesus was very tempted to not have the human experience. In his dance with the devil in the desert, Jesus was offered the chance to go around the human experience, avoiding all of the pain and anguish that come with our existence. But Jesus replied that he would like to have the whole experience, and indeed he did and then some.

Isn't that what we are all here for, to have the whole experience? Christ's example is truly worth emulating, whether we count ourselves as Christians or not. This life is not preparation for something else. This is the reason we were brought into existence by our Creator, to live this life and experience all of its fullness, sweetness, richness, and yes, pain and suffering, too. We were not put here to just "get through" to some sweet bye and bye on the other side, as seductive as that idea can be, especially in our most regressive moments.

Some of these regressive periods come when we're feeling most tired and discouraged by the slings and arrows of daily misfortune. But these times can also create openings for new insights. I was in an airport years ago, tired and exhausted, when I noticed a clock on the wall that had stopped. I thought, of all the places in the world to have a stopped clock! I looked at my watch and I glanced back at the clock and I had one of those reflective moments. I thought, "You know, that clock is exactly right, twice a day, if only for one second each time." Was that reassuring? I considered that my trusty watch, no matter how faithfully it ticked along, was probably never exactly right. If I measured my watch against some official atomic clock somewhere that always knows "the time," then my watch was surely always off by seconds, if not minutes.

I concluded that I would rather take the living reality of my personal watch any day over the dead certainty of an airport clock, hanging on the wall with all the energy and relevance of a dead idol. And that is what I also prefer in my religion. I want a religion that will promote the living experience, fraught as it is with anxiety and the unknown, over the dead certainty of a religion that offers no opportunity for personal growth and transformation.

When we accept a living reality, we give ourselves a greater degree of freedom to keep the sacraments alive, even if it means changing the theology. The 1928 Prayer Book of the Episcopal Church, for example, includes a baptismal rite prayer, "The Ministration of Holy Baptism," that used to contain the line, "Do you renounce the world, the devil and the flesh?"

This line was removed because it came to be viewed as anachronistic. Who would want to renounce the world that we live in, that we are part of? The liturgy implied that we were not worthy to gather up the crumbs under the table. That's bad theology. If we're not worthy, then what are we doing here? Unfortunately, the Roman Catholic Church seems determined to perpetuate this viewpoint, in 2006 revising a pre-Communion prayer (part of a larger revision of its Mass to supposedly return it closer to the original Latin) to read, "Lord, I am not worthy that you should enter my roof."

This brings up another malady of modern American life: low self-esteem. Too many of our religious leaders seem to share the mind-set of Mr. Marks, the tyrannical accountant in *The Producers*, who declared when he detected a whiff of autonomy among his minions, "Do I smell the revolting stench of self-esteem?"

An entirely separate book could and should be written about this pervasive problem, but let me suffice to say here that, in my 35 years as priest and analyst, I've hardly seen a soul come into my office who wasn't suffering from low self-esteem, which is basically a person's subjective appraisal of himself as not good enough, not worthy, and certainly not competent enough to make his own major life decisions.

Is fundamentalism a major contributing factor to low self-esteem, or does it simply exploit this human weakness along with anxiety and fear of death? The answer is both, and the tragedy is that American religion is failing to fulfill a sorely needed function, which is to help each person develop a healthy, positive self-image.

## DIVINE ANXIETY

Paradoxically, anxiety is both that which drives us toward the sacred and the symbols, and that which makes the symbols diabolic. It is an irony. We need the symbolic life to help manage the anxiety, to have some sense that we're not alone in this, that these questions I'm asking have been asked before, or that there are different answers and ways to respond that can serve as guideposts in my journey.

Despite the false promise of fundamentalism, anxiety is inevitable even for those who seek to enter the kingdom of God. But there are different kinds of anxiety. There is sick, or pathological anxiety, but there is also divine anxiety. This second type of anxiety is the unavoidable price of admittance to the kingdom, because all who enter are consciously choosing to individuate and separate from the group, which we'll explore at length in chapter four.

Embracing the divine anxiety that comes with living in the kingdom of God means accepting the consequences and responsibilities of choice. This anxiety is a positive sign, because it signals to us that we are growing and not stuck. It means that we have evicted ourselves from a place of comfort—another word would be *stagnation*—and are entering the realm of mystery called the unknown, where exhilarating new possibilities await.

Jesus weighed in on this journey, telling us to "Enter by the narrow gates, because the road that leads to perdition is very wide and many take it. It's a hard road that leads to life and only a few find it."

This has been interpreted in many ways, perhaps most widely as "don't drink, don't smoke, and don't follow the highway to the whorehouse." Others, such as the Jungian analyst and Episcopal priest John Sanford, have interpreted the wide road to perdition as being the route most of us take through life, which is to remain unconscious. The superhighway of unconsciousness is the safe and easy way, the route of least resistance and mass identity preferred by the great majority of the population.

Jesus said, "Many are called, but few are chosen." I believe he was referring to the new consciousness required to enter the kingdom of God, and I would add, "Many are called, but few choose."

The narrow road is the path of consciousness, which requires close and constant attention, lest we veer off into the ditch of unconsciousness (which even the most conscious among us inevitably do, but thankfully the resurrectional grace of the Christian myth teaches us that a new beginning is always available to us).

The narrowness of the gates suggests anxiety is part of the process of finding the kingdom, for narrowness and anxiety have long been associated, as both are highly constrictive by nature. Narrowness here does not imply a narrow, fundamentalist point of view, but the kind of narrowness that requires focus, discernment, and dedication to a long and arduous process.

There are no concrete certainties in the kingdom, which is to say there are no dead certainties. Nor will one find the beguiling sentimentality of fundamentalism there, for the overly sentimental "sweet Jesus" religion of the literalists is one inch from its opposite, which is brutality. Pushed far enough, this sweet religion quickly flips and becomes brutal as hell. The fundamentalists who want you to know their sweet, gentle savior so desperately will kill you if you don't receive him.

The false promise is that you will receive so many joyous, graceful benefits when you "take Jesus" into your life, but the fact is there is no grace without disgrace, and there is no Easter without Good Friday. What I'm working toward is that there is no free entry into the kingdom, and what must be sacrificed—you've probably guessed it by now—is the ego. Or, more precisely, it is the ego's supremacy which must be sacrificed so that the Self may take its proper place in the kingdom of God.

Among all the deaths we experience, the biological death is probably the least challenging. Everybody seems to be able to do that. But the death of the ego is a very difficult one. Many are called but few choose to make this death-dealing, life-giving sacrifice, and the few who have managed to become their own autonomous authorities certainly have not been encouraged to do so by our existing religious structures.

The tragedy of using the Christian myth as an authoritarian fear tactic to keep people subordinate and infantilized seems to me to be the real evil, rather than those sundry sins railed against in pulpits across the nation. It is as if we have given these religious structures the authority to act as our mothers and fathers, and not very good ones. On a very deep and primitive level, we have.

## CHAPTER 3

# THE CHURCH AS NEGATIVE MOTHER AND FATHER

Skating on the thin ice of heresy, which is where I often seem to find myself, I've said that the church is a prostitute, but she is also my mother.

We yearn for the church to be our mother, a calling she willingly accepts and inevitably carries out with all the good intentions and imperfections of a human mother. I acknowledge the Christian church as my mother, the matrix in which I was formed and nurtured. She's given me many gifts, including a sacred story and set of symbols that imbue my life with meaning and connect me to a larger mystery. My mother church gives me sanctuary from the nightmare and burden that Chekhov spoke of, and for that gift I am forever grateful.

At the same time, my mother church has become a prostitute for selling her soul—her living water—to the culture for money, power, and prestige. The church has also largely failed us as a father, if you consider the father's most important archetypal function, which is to empower us and show us how to be in the world as independent, autonomous adults. I don't say these things to be provocative, but to hopefully get us to take a more mature, realistic, and balanced view of the humanity of the church.

No institution on earth has been a more problematic parental figure than the church, which has willingly exploited our mother and father complexes by creating a system of reward and punishment that fosters dependency while discouraging maturity and autonomy. This system has become so insidiously efficient that we too often confuse pleasing God, or following God's will, with what we are really trying to do, which is to quiet the voice of the complex and ease its painful psychic tension.

It was Jung who developed the term *complex*, or "feeling-toned complex of ideas," as a way of mapping or conceptualizing the psyche. A complex is a split-off part of the psyche, a cluster of unconscious feelings and beliefs with an autonomous energy source that can be activated by any number of stimuli, even an innocuous remark or look that appears negative or critical when interpreted through the filter of the complex. When a complex is activated, it expresses itself in thoughts and actions that can be puzzling to ourselves and others, such as an irrational outburst or a collapse into self-pity or self-criticism.

The most widespread complex, if you count up how many times it's mentioned in popular culture, would seem to be the inferiority complex. But even the inferiority complex is a mother or father complex at heart. Because the relationship with the mother and father is the primary and most formative relationship of our life—setting the stage for all future relationships—it's hardly surprising that these complexes cause some of our most dysfunctional behavior and attitudes toward ourselves.

Each complex has its own voice, core belief, feeling tone, and attitude. For many people, the voice of the mother complex is the plaintive plea that "It's not safe out there," or "The world's too big, and I'm too small." This voice arrives with the seductive, regressive, and ultimately destructive temptation to retreat from the call of a larger life and crawl back into the figurative womb. For just as many, the father complex announces itself with a stern "You're not good enough," or "You'll never measure up." The core belief is you're never far from getting your ass kicked, or kicked out, by this shaming and punishing voice.

These are generalizations, though, since each complex is as individual as the psyche in which it lives. But at their most basic level, the complexes invariably boil down to "Good boy" or "Bad girl," answering our primal need for approval, or if that is not available, then at least knowing the rules so we can correct our behavior. This most fundamental human longing is what has been exploited by religious authority structures.

A little background on archetypes and how we project them can help us gain a deeper understanding of the mother and father complexes and their relationship to the church. Jung developed the idea of archetypes as templates for our deepest human needs and longings. In religion, he said, the archetypes are humanity's God makers and faith givers, and we also have archetypes for mother, father, heroes, and villains. The archetypes are aspects of the collective unconscious, that part of the transpersonal unconscious shared by all humankind.

Because we are largely unconscious of the archetypal predispositions inside of us, we project our deepest feelings, fears, and longings outward onto people, institutions, and events. We also project our shadow, that dark part of ourselves that we refuse to consciously recognize. The archetypes are thus mirrored back to us from the objects of our outward projection, helping us to access their power and energy. If we are conscious enough, they may also help us to recognize these dimensions within our own psyche.

Two of the strongest archetypes are mother and father, and we project these archetypes onto our biological parents, most naturally, but also onto spouses, mentors, companies, and governments. We make some of our most powerful projections of mother and father onto the church, which indeed has a potentially positive parental function to fulfill in providing us with a sense of love, nurturance, and the ability to secure our place in a world that is often threatening and overwhelming.

As we mature, we can project the mother and father archetypes onto persons and institutions with a greater degree of consciousness, which is to say that we are aware of the projection and its limits. With this approach, we can take great sustenance and comfort in accessing the mother or father energy that is available all around us, while at the same time remaining conscious of the limits of the projection and the reality that no entity can ever completely fulfill our tremendous archetypal need for mother and father.

The projections become unhealthy and regressive when we unconsciously and neurotically cling to mother and father figures, including our own parents, expecting to receive the self-love and empowerment we can ultimately only provide for ourselves—if and when we grow up and become mature, autonomous adults.

As most of us know, there are plenty of parents and surrogates out there who will all too gladly serve their own neurotic needs by conspiring with our mother and father complexes. They do so to hook us and keep us dependent. How many stories have we heard about the suffocating mother who discourages her child from growing up, lest she be lonely or no longer have a purpose? Or the father who continually shames the child into believing he will never be good enough, trapping the child in a doomed cycle of futile attempts to please?

## MOTHER

What to do about the mother? The solution is not for our biological and institutional mothers to try to become better mothers. For the most part, they're already doing the best they can. The problem has never been with the mother, but with her inability to fulfill the maternal archetype that is projected onto her. No mere human or human institution can possibly fulfill this deep, eternal longing, so any projection will inevitably lead to disappointment and disillusion.

My own biological mother, God rest her soul, was a depressed young woman from a small town in western Arkansas, struggling to learn how to care for a two-year-old son. My father was a traveling salesman who was often away working the territory, so her depression was often aggravated by feelings of loneliness and helplessness.

Neither my mother nor any woman, no matter how educated or sophisticated she was, could possibly provide for me the archetypal energy of the eternal mother who gestates and gives birth to all life in creation. The mother is the primary creative force of the universe, even though our Christian God image describes this as a masculine act. She soothes the ego's greatest fear, that of nonbeing, by bringing forth life where none existed before. She promotes growth and healing and is the essence of *salvo*, the nurturing salve that is the root word for salvation.

We all long for the experience of mothering or being mothered. From our cellular level, we are driven toward the nurturance, connectedness, relatedness, and containment that mother provides, and without which we wouldn't survive. Johnson describes the feminine qualities of the mother as coming from the left side of the heart, the shield side, which symbolizes gestation, birth, nourishment, and the rhythms of the seasons.

The yearning for mother is so strong that we will try to make a mother out of anything through our projections. The leading Roman Catholic university in this country is called Notre Dame, "Our Mother." We refer to our schools and churches as alma maters, Latin for "nourishing mother." Even our high-tech world has kept up with this primal instinct, giving us the motherboard as the most basic element of the computer. And it may come as a shock to you, but I've had men in my practice who try to make mothers out of their spouses!

The need for connection with mother is wired down to the instinctual level in primates. There are stories of wild dogs mothering other species, even humans, and gorillas projected their mother hunger onto Dian Fossey. In the famous Terrycloth Experiment, rhesus monkeys were separated from their mothers at birth in order to research the theory of early attachment. The monkeys were offered the choice of a soft surrogate mother made of terrycloth and foam, but with no milk, or a wire frame with a rubber nipple. The babies chose the dry but soft mother, suggesting that the need for comfort and nurturance, even if from an inanimate object, is stronger than the need for food.

So while I try to be realistic about the dark side of the church, there's also a positive side, and that is that the religion of your choice or experience or background can provide for you those things that we expect from the mother. As we project that archetype onto her, sometimes she can fulfill some of those needs, albeit in a limited way.

The mother herself lives with an eternal and unconscious conflict, which is birthing and nurturing the helpless and totally dependent child, followed by a second birthing wherein the child ceases to depend on her. Because gestation, birth, and nurture are so much a part of the mother, she is often reluctant to give up these functions, lest she slide into nonbeing herself. A good mother gives her children both roots and wings. She provides an early foundation of being valued, instills a healthy sense of self, and gives them a sense of belonging. But she must also do the opposite, which is to let her children go—a duty that is too much to ask of some mothers.

The dark side of the mother therefore is possessiveness, consumption, and infantilization, and Johnson adds malice, revenge, irrationality, and wrath. While the positive mother pushes the fledgling out of the nest, the negative mother works to foster dependency. That's the smother mother we hear so much about. Many might consider that old saying, "The hand that rocks the cradle rules the world," to be a tribute to the importance of motherhood, but consider the darker implications as well.

The biological mother gives the child a mixed message. "You cannot live without me," she says. At the same time she adds, "If you stay here I will kill you." In the parlance of clinical psychology, that's what we call a conflict.

Mothers like the idea of somebody being dependent on them because that is their first experience of mothering, that symbiosis in the womb. In the early development of the infant, all they hear is "Mama," and they cherish that ecstatic inflation of having the humbling, awe-inspiring vocation of mother. Many young girls with low self-esteem are drawn to premature motherhood, figuring, "I don't know who I am in the world or what I can do, but I do know one thing I can do, and that is to mother." Our fellow creatures seem to have a much easier time of letting go than us humans, even if they give birth the minute they hit puberty. A mother duck, for example, doesn't have this neurotic need for her ducklings to define her life for her.

To give up the validating identity of motherhood is difficult for most mothers, so the dark side of mothering, which is to consume and possess, is often pursued with great motivation. It's usually done with sweetness and niceness, as in the fairy tale of Hansel and Gretel, where the children are enticed into the witch's grasp by a gingerbread house with a candy cane roof. That sweetness brings them into the possessiveness of the negative mother, who plops them into the oven and consumes them. Even my own grandmother used to say, "Oh Pittman, you are so sweet I could eat you with a spoon"—a hint that the darker side of the mother unconsciously resides within even the most benign and well-intentioned women.

The same modern advances that have created so much anxiety have also separated us from nature, our original archetypal mother. Mother Nature, as we still call her, was the wellspring of so many of the pagan religions, which centered around celebrating the earth and its seasons. Beginning with Judaism and continuing with Christianity and Islam, the Abrahamic monotheistic religions have nearly wiped out all traces of the feminine from our spiritual lives, aggravating our mother hunger while at the same time exploiting it.

Having lost our connection to the mothering energy of nature and instinct, we have perverted mother (*mater*) into matter, or material, setting the stage for the modern malady of materialism, which in turn is so tied up with the American civil religion and its capitalistic values. We clearly we live in a culture of great spiritual impoverishment, Hollis has written, with addictive materialism making us slaves to surfaces.

We seek to fill our emptiness with material, but it is a futile pursuit. If we took all the merchandise from every megamall and strip center in America and threw it into our starved collective psyches, it would hardly make a dent. We would just be piling up more mountains of monetary debt on top of our tremendous spiritual deficit, and we will still be hungry ghosts. There isn't enough matter on earth to fulfill our deep need for *mater*, and institutionalized religion has used this all-consuming hunger—the dark side of the mother archetype—to keep us infantilized and dependent.

The negative mother does not want us to have a new idea, because we might come to a new way of thinking, and heaven forbid, grow up and leave home. Under the thumb of the negative mother, we suffer self-alienation when some nascent inner authority urges us to a new thought or attitude. If we begin to consider a novel idea that might lead us to act differently in the twenty-first century, the voice of a negative mother, still stuck in the first century, could well lead to an overwhelming feeling of guilt. So too often we stay in the religious structure out of a neurotic dependence, and that's been part of the self-perpetuating nature of the church. If you never have any graduates, then you've always got a market.

## FATHER

Now to the father. The two main functions of the father archetype are to help us separate from the mother and to civilize our primitive instincts. As Johnson writes, the masculine, or right side, of the brain is positively associated with action, protection, benevolent justice, lucid luminous reason, and sunlike creative power.

In its separating function, the role of the father is to empower, to provide a presence, a voice and an attitude that says, "Let me show you a world that you can live in without your mother. Let me help you separate from her."

In her studies of indigenous tribes in New Guinea, the anthropologist Margaret Mead came across a ritual wherein the mothers of the village would gather all the adolescent boys into a hut and stay with them until the adult males arrived to abduct their younger counterparts. The mothers would feign terror and pretend to faint, in effect giving up their conscious presence over the boys so that the males could spirit them out of the hut (a womb symbol) and initiate them into manhood.

This may sound primitive to us, but as a ritual, it has a sound basis. In effect, it says very clearly to the boys, "I, the father, am here to separate you from her and free you from these confines. If you stay here she will kill you, but I'm here to teach you how to live in the world without her."

The great enemy of human consciousness is anxiety, which boils down to the fear of being overwhelmed or abandoned. Even those of us who had the most stable upbringings and the best possible parents are not immune to the familiar feeling that life's too big and I'm too small. We all need to be empowered, to have guides to lead us and teach us to be competent and confident in the world. That is the role of the father, whose work cannot begin until the child is separated from the mother.

A second role of the paternal archetype is to civilize, a process Robert Johnson describes as "the brightest achievement of mankind (which) consists of culling out those characteristics that are dangerous to the smooth functioning of our ideals."

God knows we need structure. We long for a father to establish limits, just as we long for the mother's nurturing. It is important for the wisdom of the elders to be passed on, and the wisdom is, "These are norms for human behavior. This is what works in our culture. And this is what's abnormal. This doesn't work in our culture." To which we can respond, "Thank you, it's helpful to know that there are limitations to what we can do if our culture is to survive."

One of the things that most religions are interested in is the idea of grace, forgiveness, and transformation through acceptance and love. We depend on the positive father to determine the appropriate balance of setting limits on behavior in order to survive as a culture and offering up grace and forgiveness. I've often reflected on the fact that Pope John Paul II, the Bishop of Rome, publicly forgave the Turkish assassin who shot and wounded him three days after the shooting, asking Catholics to "pray for my brother, whom I have sincerely forgiven." The Pope later visited the man in prison and also visited his family. Even with the Pope's forgiveness, the man was not released from prison until he had served much of his term, and shortly after his release, he was rearrested. The point is that we have to be realistic about the boundaries and limits of human behavior and forgiveness. The father can teach us to be not cynical, but realistic.

In Western religion, the father archetype has been much stronger than that of the mother. We call ordained people "Father," sometimes regardless of their gender. When I first called an ordained woman onto the staff of the cathedral where I was dean, one of the parishioners insisted on calling her "Father." This would be a good place to point out that the archetypes are not gender specific. Often they are, but men can mother, and women can father. In fact, some of the best mothers I know are men, and vice versa.

The positive father in religions affirms our worth, telling us that we are important, that we belong and we are cared for. The problem is that when we project our need for father onto the hierarchy of the church, we are just begging for somebody to provide structure for us so we don't have to be anxious. We want a father to tell us what to think, how to feel, and how to act.

As it does with the negative mother, the church is all too ready to rush in and exploit this archetypal longing. The positive side of the paternal archetype quickly flips to become the negative father, who is punishing and exclusionary. The dark side of the father is rigid and arid, as devoid of life force as the desert. Johnson associates this side with cruel justice, cold unfeeling malice, and unplayful moral force.

The legalistic mind-set of the negative father is obsessed with enforcing the black-and-white, always/never letter of the law, never making room for the expression of novelty or individuality. Few of us have escaped the punitive wrath of the negative father in our lives, whether it's being sent to our bedrooms, forced to eat our vegetables, or banished from tribe, church, or household. Apart from being sent to hell, the ultimate punishment in religion is excommunication, where an unfortunate soul is prohibited from receiving a sacrament because they've broken the rules.

The exclusionary voice of the father tells us who is in and who is out, which is to say who has earned God's grace and the reward of heaven. Exclusion can be much more subtle than casting someone into the fire and brimstone, but it can be just as painful.

When I was the dean of Christ Church Cathedral in Houston, we used to have a cartoon on the bulletin board that pictured the tight-lipped American Gothic couple. The wife was saying to her husband, "Don't speak to them, Henry. They don't go to our church." We can appreciate the humor, but too many of us have felt the painful sting of being excluded from a family, group, or even a conversation because we are somehow different.

Punishment, exclusion, and legalism—these are interesting sorts of behavior patterns for a Gospel of grace and peace, are they not? Even if we grew up with the most loving, passive father, most of us have the self-loathing, self-judging voice of the negative father within us, because we have it in spades in our culture. It is no wonder that the dominant party in American politics, which some have called our only national party, has such a militant, toe-the-line attitude that tells us to love it or leave it, to shut up and fall into line. Most of all, don't question, because if you disagree with us, you're unpatriotic. This negative father voice can be seen everywhere in our culture, in sports, education, business—and most of all in our American religion.

The most adolescent viewpoint espoused by negative father exclusivity is to claim that only certain people are going to heaven, wherever that may be and whatever that may mean in the twenty-first century. Just think about what this heaven would be like. Only one-third of the world is Christian, so two-thirds of the world is excluded from the outset. Of the Christian third, one-third thinks the other two-thirds isn't going to heaven because they are

Roman Catholic, Mormon, or otherwise disqualified. And of the one-ninth of the world that thinks it's going to heaven, there are so many deep theological schisms, so much finger-pointing and blame, that we're left with only a few percent of the world's most judgmental, rigid, and exclusionary people going to heaven. I surely wouldn't want to take a car trip to El Paso with them, much less have them as my companions for eternity!

## THE SHADOW OF THE CHURCH

Another reason the church has been so wounding to so many people is because it has not owned its shadow, or dark side. In Jungian psychology, the *shadow* refers to those dark parts of ourselves that we refuse to consciously recognize. Johnson describes the shadow as those "refused and unacceptable characteristics (that) do not go away; they only collect in the dark corners of our personality." Calling the shadow "the despised quarter of our being," Johnson notes that it has a tremendous store of energy, nearly as much as the ego. He writes that if the shadow ever begins to act autonomously, that is outside the control of the ego, it has the potential to become "a terrible monster in our psychic house."[1]

Institutions as well as individuals have shadows, and there is ample evidence that the shadow of the church has grown ominously dark and powerful. The shadow may not be in total control of the church's psychic house, but we can see disturbing flare-ups of this pent-up darkness when it comes to our most contentious social issues.

It would be enormously beneficial if the church would begin to own its shadow, acknowledging the harm it causes by colluding with our complexes and playing out the roles of negative mother and father. There is little chance of that happening, so we must do for ourselves what Christ commanded and kill our mother and father—symbolically, of course.

If we are to grow up, we must acknowledge that we have conspired with the church to create this neurotic, dependent symbiosis. We have projected our needs onto the mother church and expected her to fix us and take care of us. We create the same kind of projections with other institutions as well. From the "nanny state" to "Ma Bell," we have expected large, powerful structures to take fulfill our needs. The reality is that these people and institutions can't and won't take care of us. They are just not capable of it. They have failed us always, and we can hardly blame them, because even if they have tried to seduce us with sugary gingerbread house, we entered of our own free will.

If anybody ever got a whiff of the truly liberating message of the Gospel, they'd be free, and the last thing they would want to do is belong to a church whose primary mission seems to be to keep people from growing up. I don't mean that literally, of course. There are important things a conscious, affirming church has to offer, such as ritual process, community, and helping us access the transcendent energy of sacred stories and symbols. But a free person would no longer willingly go to a church out of a superstitious fear of punishment or an obligation to legalism.

So, how to free ourselves of the parental projections we make onto the church? Instinctively, we all know the answer in the back of the book, and that is that each of us must ultimately become our own mother—and father. It is as simple, and as difficult, as growing up.

## CHAPTER 4

# How Does Religion Wound Us?

At this point, the reader may have noticed that I'm a little bit concerned about fundamentalism and its growing influence in the American religious landscape. Before moving on to the second half of this book, toward a more hopeful and positive view of religion and the liberating and transformative message of the Gospel, I want to make clear that my objection to fundamentalism is not just that it's not my cup of tea, or that it seems to me to be anti-intellectual, contrary to exercising our God-given ability to reason. As an Anglican and a Jungian, I try to always make a conscious effort to stay away from elitism, or getting into an us-versus-them viewpoint.

Nor is my objection to fundamentalism founded in its substantial punitive and exclusionary streaks. Many systems, including our legal system, have these qualities, and it would be irresponsible to argue that they are all bad.

My concern about fundamentalism is that it is harmful, a realization that started to dawn on me about halfway into my career as a priest, when I began to see that "That Old-Time Religion" wasn't just not good enough for me, but that it's not good enough for anybody. In contrast to true religion, fundamentalism is a sadistic pathology that has hijacked Christianity's sacred story and set of symbols, misusing these substantial resources to control people through fear and perpetuate its own power.

Fundamentalism is unhealthy because it destroys human personality and creativity, one of the most accessible realms through which we can all encounter divine transcendence. This dangerous mutation of religion also hurts people through shame, punishment, and exclusion. Its viewpoint is so rigid, extreme, and unbalanced that it quickly flips and becomes its opposite. Push this seemingly sweet and sentimental religion far enough, and it becomes ruthless and brutal.

The fundamentalist in any religion says, "We have a God of love we want you to know, and if you do not accept him, He will kill you. Or we will." This is why so many horrific acts are committed in the name of God, from terrorism to the murder of doctors who provide abortions. Spectacular acts of violence capture headlines and occasionally penetrate our thickened skins, but millions of more subtle acts of violence go unreported and unnoticed every day—acts of exclusion and punishment directed at those who do not conform, even if they are among our closest loved ones.

Fundamentalism is also harmful to the larger, collective society, especially a society such as ours, with its emergent pluralism. But as a mental health professional and priest, my main concern is looking at how fundamentalism affects individual minds and souls.

I've talked earlier about how one of the most visible effects of fundamentalist religion is that it infantilizes its followers. What exactly does infantilization mean, and what are the consequences? Being infantilized means getting stuck at an immature stage of the natural maturation process, which unfolds in three natural phases, and the consequences are never growing up to become a full adult, with all of the exhilarating independence and autonomy that implies.

For the first seven years of a child's life, the parents are the authority figures, which is natural and normal from a developmental psychology point of view.

In the second stage of life, from about the age of 7 to 14, the peer group becomes the most influential authority in the child's life. The immature ego knows that it must separate from the parents, and transferring authority to the peer group becomes a safe and easy intermediary step, because strict conformity is still required. Anyone who has ever witnessed a teenager's slavish adherence to the norms of the peer group knows this immutable law very well.

The third developmental phase, beginning in the mid-to-late teens, is becoming your own authority, which means granting yourself an increasing degree of autonomy in how you think and act.

Of course, these stages are general guidelines for development, as we don't automatically switch to the next stage when we reach a certain age. More realistically, growing up psychologically is a generally linear process where we gradually move onto the next stage and develop its characteristics as we get older, but we can all have regressive periods where we take two steps forward and one step back, no matter what our age or level of consciousness.

There's an old story about three umpires, which illustrates the three stages of maturation and the evolution of claiming one's authority. In this story, a cub newspaper reporter interviews these umpires, asking each to describe how he knows whether it's a ball or a strike.

The rookie umpire says, "It couldn't be easier. I just look in the book—the book tells me exactly what I need to know."

Next he asks the journeyman umpire, who has a little more experience. "I don't know," he says. "I just calls 'em the way I see 'em."

Finally, the reporter asks the master umpire, who immediately replies, "They ain't nothing 'til I call 'em."

For most of us, who are still rookies at consciousness, it's comforting to have a book that will tell us exactly what to do in every situation. As we move a little higher on the consciousness ladder, we try to do the best we can with our hard-won experience and reason. Finally, when we assume our own authority at the master umpire level, we assert the reality that something only comes into existence for us through our viewpoint, or worldview. Just think about the profound implications of that. Far from being hubristic, this is a sober acknowledgement of the awesome responsibility we are given to choose and decide—to develop our own viewpoint about anything that happens to us.

Fundamentalism encourages people to get stuck in the first or second stages of development, to rely on a negative parental voice that says, "Don't question. Just believe. Surrender your authority to us, and we will take care of you." This devil's bargain has never been more tempting for so many, because even though the world has always been religiously diverse, thanks to the Internet and other modern methods of communications (and destruction) we have never been more aware of the world's innate plurality. Instead of seeing this as a beautiful mosaic, we see it as a threatening stream of Babel. There is just too much coming at us, making us feel overwhelmed and anxious.

If we are to create a mature and healthy twenty-first-century spirituality for ourselves, we are called on to make consciousness and build soul by living the questions and suffering the paradoxes. Most people, however, are all too eager to abdicate this responsibility to someone or something outside of ourselves, preferring to stay stuck at a level where the church, family, government, or corporation will tell us exactly what to do in every situation.

This is entirely understandable, because becoming conscious is a painful, messy, and often lonely process, but it is an enterprise we are called to accept as human beings. Fundamentalists believe they have cornered the market on defining evil, but ignoring the call to consciousness and surrendering to an authoritarian, infantilizing religious structure seems to me to be closer to the true definition of evil. As a dis-integrating force, evil is the opposite of integrating or becoming whole, which is the only way to find the Self and God. Evil as a force leads to nothingness, which is as good and concise a definition I've ever heard for hell, wherever that is and whatever it means today.

Fundamentalism causes further collateral damage by suppressing human personality and creativity. Far from being the narcissistic indulgence of a handful of elite artists, creativity is the birthright of every human being, and our greatest commission is the call to create our own lives. As children of God, this creative energy is available to us all, but when fear and anxiety keep us living within small and rigid structures, there is no room for curiosity, spontaneity, experimentation, or the joy that comes from discovering the new or the novel.

The dark side of the fundamentalist fixation on so-called normative behavior is that if you're not normal, you can't belong, when in fact the abnormal may be the novelty of God. I've always said that one of the most appealing aspects of God is novelty. In fact, if you asked me what I thought was the primary nature of God, I would have to say novelty. The opposite of the predictable or normative, *novelty* means "newness, difference, change, and evolution." In other words, it is life itself.

As Darwin wrote in *On the Origin of Species*, "endless forms most beautiful and wonderful have been, and are being, evolved." A novelty of God is often first seen as abnormal, which carries a judgmental view, when in fact it is merely new and different. In evolution, new phyla break out of the existing orders, and they are abnormal but also powerful and transformative. Novelty occurs in religion as well, and humankind has had countless thousands of God images, both evolutionary and revolutionary. Sometimes, a new God image or religion is so radical and countercultural that it is ruthlessly suppressed. Christianity, which Jung has described as a tremendous gift to humanity, was violently resisted as a novelty during the first few centuries of its existence. Unfortunately, after the Emperor Constantine gave Christianity political legitimacy in the fourth century, the institutional church became an oppressive force against novelty.

Fundamentalism also quashes our ability to solve problems, which is a key part of growing up. In premarital counseling, the first thing I say when a young couple comes into my office is, "Don't!" In all seriousness, the second thing I say is that if you are going to be married, then problems are not optional but guaranteed. And it's through solving the problems that one becomes truly married to another. Problem-solving is where the deepest and truest form of love—the love that lets the loved one be—is nurtured. It's where the deep bonds of love and trust are forged and strengthened. And it is the ultimate crucible of commitment.

It's exactly the same with our own lives. Just as we learn by solving math problems all through school, problem-solving is what helps us to grow up in the real world. If we won't take that responsibility, then we will never experience the exhilarating, soul-making possibilities that come through solving our own problems. If we abdicate the hard questions and the tough challenges to some external authority, we will retard our own development and never grow up. We will be forever dependent, never independent.

Finally, fundamentalism can destroy our relationship with ourself, which is by far the most important relationship we will ever have. Truth be told, it is the only relationship we can count on. This is not meant to sound self-centered, but the truth is that it is impossible to form a healthy relationship with another human being if our relationship with ourself is not healthy.

If you grow up believing that you're a miserable sinner, then the damage has already begun. And the idea that God sacrificed his only son—which like the concept of original sin is nowhere in the Bible—only makes the guilt worse. It's very difficult to have a healthy self-image when you believe that there is something fundamentally wrong with you, when you are convinced that, thanks to John Calvin and St. Augustine, you are born a depraved sinner and your only hope is to submit yourself to a dependent relationship with an exploitative religious structure.

In *All the King's Men*, Willie Stark, the fictional character based on legendary Louisiana governor Huey Long, says, "Man is conceived in sin and born in corruption." Some very powerful leaders in our country subscribe to this view, including former Attorney General John Ashcroft, a Pentecostal, who said, "What I have to do to please God is to confess that I am a sinner instead of trying to prove that I am good."

How much better off we would be if we had an attitude more like that of the Sufi teacher Pir Vilayat Inayat Khan, who said, "If you could see yourself through God's eyes, you wouldn't believe how beautiful you are!"

There is the tremendous cost of not claiming your own authority, and that cost is essentially your life, or at least your health or happiness. Therapists' offices are full of people who feel as though they have missed their lives, or at least huge chunks of them, and it is most acutely at midlife when the proverbial chickens come home to roost.

When I baptized my first son, I said at his sermon, "I hope the day will come when you will choose your own values, even if they are counter to mine." I was giving him permission, even when he was still an infant, to chart his own journey and make his own decisions in life. Now I have no delusion that I'm the perfect father, and Lord knows I don't want to be anyone's religious authority, but I do hope that I can help something to resonate within my own children and my fellow children of God, so that they can begin the process of individuation, which is essentially about becoming ourselves.

Perhaps the best place to begin is with love—the self-love that can only start with self-compassion. Love was Jesus' foremost command, and loving ourselves would be the greatest gift we could give to him—not to mention ourselves and our loved ones. It would be amazing how much our relationships would be transformed if we began to love ourselves, for only then would we have love to give to others. In that sense, charity really does begin at home, in the inner world.

Self-love sounds like a simple pop-psychology cure-all, perfect for a culture that craves easy fixes. But let me tell you—in all my years of people helping, it is one of the most difficult things for people to do. We have radical double standards wherein we easily forgive flaws and overlook faults in others, but we can't abide the slightest imperfection in ourselves. It seems like we never miss a chance to pass judgment on ourselves, and it all goes back to the voices of our negative mother and father complexes.

Lest we sin, we follow the rules and try to think of ourselves as moral. We want so desperately to think of ourselves as good boys and girls, when most of the time what we consider morality is nothing more than conformity out of fear. That doesn't make you moral, it just makes you a highly conformed and legalistic individual.

In our culture, the definition of good has come to mean somebody's ability to conform and adapt to normative behavior. But we know that if we push the good girl or good boy too far, then good Lord deliver us from the unbalanced outburst that may result, for these good souls are completely cut off from their shadows, or any sense of the darkness that balances lightness and makes us fully human, so it inevitably comes roaring out when provoked. At the other extreme, the shadow claims its inevitable due in more insidious and self-destructive ways, invisible to everyone but the soul being consumed.

The truest meaning of morality is not about following the rules, but about being true to yourself. The words *good* and *God* come from the same root, which means "fit for a purpose." In my house, we have two kinds of chairs, good chairs and antiques. The antiques make for good art but bad chairs, because they don't serve the end for which they were created, which is mine. So goodness is not a moral judgment or an authoritarian evaluation of one's ability to conform and adapt. Rather, is to serve that purpose for which you were created, which is to be the best possible you.

The greatest moral question then becomes, "Are you going to be you? Are you going to be your true self? Or are you going to be what people or society want you to be?" This view of morality gets to the very essence of that highest of Christian values—atonement—"at-one-ment"—which is about nothing other than becoming a whole and integrated human being, at one with oneself.

What about sin? It comes from the Greek word *hamartia*, which is found in the New Testament, and it means "to be off the mark." So we can begin to see that sin too really means not being true to yourself. It means not responding to the call of your true Self, which Joseph Campbell phrased so elegantly as "following your bliss."

Bliss sounds very blissful, and the way of consciousness is indeed the road to the paradise that awaits in the kingdom of God. But the road will not be easy, which is why many are called but few choose. And the cost of becoming yourself is dear, a mounting sum of potential anxiety, abandonment, judgment, misunderstanding, and loneliness for refusing to go the way of the family or larger culture. Just ask anyone whose calling places them at odds against the majority religion, political party, sexual orientation, or even the family business. Any kind of autonomy is countercultural, and self-perpetuating systems do not respond favorably when their survival is threatened. Sometimes the price is your life. Just ask Jesus Christ, our ultimate role model for authentic Selfhood.

Claiming your own authority is neither free nor easy, but it is a bargain and a walk in the park compared to the ultimate price that will be paid for not doing so. It bears repeating what Jung said, that the only sin is to remain unconscious. On the deepest level, our true vocation is to become ourselves, and I don't think anything would be more pleasing to the man who said, "You will do far greater things than I have." I'm speaking of Jesus Christ, of course, who has given us a beautiful model for transcendence, grace, and recognizing the divinity within ourselves and each of our fellow human beings.

PART II

# Finding a Healthy Spirituality for the Twenty-first Century

## CHAPTER 5

# RECLAIMING RELIGION

If we are to begin a discussion about what a healthy spirituality for the twenty-first century might look like, a good first step would be to reclaim the word *religion*. Though I have preached at length about the need to assert our own decision-making authority, deciding whether we are religious *or* spiritual is often not so much a conscious decision as an unconscious split. If we take a look at the etymological roots of *religion*, we can see a compelling reason for evolving from "I'm not religious, I'm spiritual" toward the more holistic attitude of "I'm both religious *and* spiritual." There's no need to settle for ors and buts in our religious and spiritual lives—not when our birthright is to have it all.

The Latin verb *ligare* means to connect, and *religare* means to reconnect. From *religare* we get *religio* and hence *religion*, which helps us to see that religion came into being to reconnect that which was once connected but has become disconnected, alienated, and estranged. The religious function is to bind, to reconnect, and to put ourselves back together again. Religion is about that universal desire, that archetypal impulse of all humans to make ourselves whole again, heal our conflicts, and reintegrate the split-off parts of ourselves that deform our souls and drive our neuroses, which Jung described as those inner cleavages that put us in a constant state of war with ourselves.

How did we ever get to be so un-whole, so broken, in the first place? There's no reason to blame ourselves or anyone else, for to be human is to be ridden with complexes and divided against ourselves. Suffering is an inescapable part of the human experience, but there is a big difference between conscious and unconscious suffering. When we suffer consciously, religion offers us a framework that can lead to healing, growth, and transcendence.

John Shelby Spong, the former Episcopal bishop of New Jersey and pro-lific (and prophetic) author, finds in Jesus's own words the liberating message that the hallmarks of the kingdom of God are not victory or righteousness, but rather the removal of those symptoms of human brokenness. Christ's teaching that the deaf will hear, the blind will see, and the lame will walk in the kingdom of God "is a portrait of the presence of God in human life that manifests itself in wholeness."[1]

If we turn Jesus's teaching inward, our broken limbs and failed organs mirror our fractured psyches and sickened souls. Our inner pain creates an-guish that is equal to or greater than our physical pain, but while we have made tremendous strides in both physiological and psychoactive medicine since Christ's day, we have still not invented an inner healing agent with as much efficacious potential as religion. It is truly miraculous that we can reattach limbs and graft arteries back together, but we seem to have actually gone backward in our ability to mend our shattered souls and psyches, with all due respect to Prozac and its peers.

The great division of our lives is consciousness/unconsciousness, result-ing in the complexes that are responsible for so much of our self-limiting and self-punishing behavior. No matter how healthy and balanced our childhoods were, regardless of how loving and supportive our parents were and are, to be human is to have complexes. The measure of our mental health and matu-rity is not whether we have complexes, but how well we are able to integrate them into consciousness, so that they lose much of their energy and we are able to remain as conscious and present as possible when they are activated.

Most people think of complexes as those brief outbursts that are usually followed by a sheepish apology, and then it's over until the next time. But complexes are actually much more insidious than that. They are chronic, low-grade, and often lifelong viewpoints we have about ourselves. They con-strict and limit our lives, and too often keep us from living our lives alto-gether. The good news is that while we so often treat complexes as if they were eternal certainties, they will usually fall apart if we can only bring them to consciousness through self-examination and analysis.

A man who almost missed his life was a patient of mine several years ago. A highly successful lawyer, this middle-aged man had been deeply unhappy for many years, if not for the bulk of his life, because he hated his profes-sion and secretly yearned to teach history and coach football at a boy's prep school. When I asked him what was stopping him from pursuing his dream, he said, "Because it would kill my father, and my wife would die."

His father was also a high-powered attorney, as his grandfather had been, so this man felt an incapacitating guilt over the very idea of leaving the fam-ily profession. Further complicating this man's feeling of being trapped, his wife had become accustomed to the lifestyle and social stature made possible by his huge salary, and he felt certain she could not survive unless he maintained the status quo.

I encouraged him to at least broach a discussion of his deepest desires with his wife and father, instead of just living with the imagined certainty of their responses. He did so and was surprised if not completely shocked by their responses. His father said, "Son, that sounds wonderful. I wish I had done something like that a long time ago. I've always hated being a lawyer." To his amazement, his wife was even more supportive. "You've been so unhappy and hard to live with all these years, I'd make any sacrifice if it would make you happy," she said.

And so the world lost a miserable lawyer but gained a happy teacher and coach, supported by a proud father and a loving wife. This is a true story, but it's also very sentimental, where everything works out in the end. Most of the time, life doesn't offer up such a Hollywood ending. The key is to love yourself enough to take the risk, even when there are no guarantees of the outcome.

I said in the previous chapter that the price of being yourself and living your life is often rejection, judgment, and misunderstanding from family and society. To expand on that, the strongest initial adversary to growth comes from our own inner critic, which speaks through the complex. We often project the voice of the complex onto other people, such as the lawyer's projection onto his father and wife. Neurotic from what Oprah Winfrey so memorably calls "the disease to please," we convince ourselves that we are pleasing and serving others by staying stuck in our self-defeating patterns, when what we are actually doing is serving the complex.

The religious aspect of the psyche can be a very positive force for healing, reconnecting, and reintegrating. This force will guide us toward evolution, individuation, and wholeness, if we are willing and able to hear and heed the voice of the Self, our inner divine nature, above the constant chatter of our complexes.

Jung said that if the church really took itself seriously, it would function as a psychotherapeutic system, and I would like to explore the healing resources that such a psycho-religious system has to offer us. Jung identified the unconscious as the seat of humankind's religious impulse, arising from life-giving contact with the *numinous*, a word he loved to use to describe the intense, divine fire that has the power to animate our lives and sustain our existence. When we see religion as the natural child of the unconscious, we honor the spontaneous, archetypal generation of our symbols, sacred stories, and God images.

Jung demanded that we humans admit that we are religious to and in our core. More recently, the Jungian analyst and priest John Dourley said that the God-making tendency is central to humankind, and that we are only fooling ourselves if we believe we have a godless option. "These same energies that express themselves in religious symbol, creed and rite, when discredited in any particular form simply reappear in some other equally absolute and potentially destructive 'ism,'" he writes.[2]

All -isms aside, the kind of religion I'm interested in is synonymous with spirituality, yet I have a need—perhaps just a personal need, I'll admit—for maintaining the word *religion* in our vocabulary as a way of recognizing and honoring the religious nature of the psyche.

I get it when people say, "I'm not religious, I'm spiritual." I understand that. But if we delve just a little deeper beyond this widespread catchphrase, I think what people really mean is that they don't buy into the dogma, creedal formulations, rules, exclusivity, and other unhealthy manifestations of organized religion that have been so limiting, wounding, and punitive.

The "I'm not religious, I'm spiritual" person is saying: "I'm not interested in the structure or rules of any particular creed or denomination, but yearn for transcendence, transformation, and life-sustaining truth. I'm interested in the meaning that comes from experiencing the divine nature of life. I long to feel connected to God, for God is love, and without love this life is hardly worth living."

What would it mean to be both spiritual *and* religious? It would include all of the above, plus the very useful idea that I approach my religious quest for healing, health, and wholeness through the particular worldview of this plan called Christianity, Buddhism, Judaism, Islam, or fill in the blank. To have a religion means to have an organizing framework through which I can view this vast and complicated world. A religion is my spiritual inheritance from my tribe, my clan, my people. As a Christian, I like to think of Christianity as a dreamstory that has been dreamt by my extended family, and this beautiful dream provides me with a set of living symbols and sacred stories through which I can live out my religious nature.

Recall what Chekhov said, that consciousness without a philosophy is no life at all, but rather a nightmare and a burden. A nightmare because without a philosophy, we have no way of making sense of a world that can often be so complex, ambiguous, and filled with violent conflict and cruel injustice. A burden because, if this life is only something to survive, to get through, then we have no hope of transcending this world and encountering the divine. Religion may not be the only resource through which we can work out our spiritual function, but it is one of the most proven, accessible, and potentially efficacious resources.

Without access to religion's healing apothecary of symbols and stories, even the most educated among us may suffer needlessly from soul sickness. A while back, I was approached by a psychiatric resident of the University of Texas medical school in Houston, and her story is a wonderful example of how our ancient sacred stories still offer healing energy that cannot be replicated by all the technology and medicine of the modern world.

This young doctor had heard that I was an Episcopal priest and Jungian psychoanalyst, and having had very little experience with religion and even less with analytical psychology, she came in for the experience of analysis, to see what this spirituality thing was all about.

First, we did our anamnesis, or the telling of her personal history, so that I could get to know her and she could also come to know herself better. She revealed that she had recently suffered a spontaneous abortion, or miscarriage, and that loss had affected her deeply. An unmarried woman, she was still laboring under a significant reactive depression from this personal tragedy and was still trying to understand what it meant and why it maintained such a grip on her. I said to her, "I think you're still in the belly of the whale, and the best thing might be for you to just sit in there for a while until you figure out what it means, and how you can heal."

Now, even in this secular age, a good number of people still know that the "belly of the whale" refers to the biblical story of Jonah, who was swallowed by this giant sea creature and spent three days in its stomach, before being spit back up onto dry land. This patient, however, had never heard of the story. She was Jewish, but she had a secular upbringing in a family that dismissed religion as irrational and of no value. When I made the reference, she looked at me in total confusion. The reference had absolutely no meaning or context for her.

Reluctant as I am to give my patients homework, I sent her home to read the book of Jonah, and when she came back the next week, we had a wonderful discussion of this sacred story and the metaphor it offers for understanding our own individual journey. Like the parable of the prodigal son, the story of Jonah has many facets, but essentially it is about individuation, or becoming ourselves. The story offers us a way to begin this long, arduous, and ultimately redeeming process, but only if we have enough patience and kindness toward ourselves to spend three days in the dark, odorous belly of a giant fish. In other words, we must be willing to suffer and sacrifice if we are to gain consciousness. The cost is dear, but the cost of doing nothing is even greater.

Deprived as she was of a religious life, with no sacred stories or symbols available as resources for gaining consciousness and understanding, this young woman had suffered tremendously in trying to comprehend the incomprehensible—why a seemingly healthy pregnancy would mysteriously self-terminate. No medical knowledge or technology could answer this question, at least not in a way that would ultimately be as healing and transformative as the one provided by the story of Jonah and the whale. What the soul needs is not medicine, but meaning. This sacred story was the key that unlocked religion as a resource for this young doctor, a resource she could use to enrich her own life and the lives of her patients and loved ones for many years to come. When the analysis ended, she gave me a tiny crystal figure of a whale which I still keep on my table of symbols, a reminder of the power of sacred story.

A reader might recall that a few chapters earlier, I criticized fundamentalist religion for trying to soothe people's anxieties by providing simple solutions for surviving in this mean old world. Religion is a valuable resource for making sense of a world that can often seem like a nightmare, but the religious traditions I trust do not encourage people to become infantilized, surrender their authority, or abdicate the hard work of becoming conscious to an external, authoritarian structure. The Gospel as I understand it encourages people do to quite the opposite, which is to recognize the awesome task it is to be free and responsible for yourself.

One reason so many spiritual people have rejected organized religion is that too many churches have become places where the divine is only talked about, rather than experienced. It's like that apocryphal church that grew up around the experience of rescuing shipwrecked people from the stormy sea but devolved into a posh club where people sit around a safe, dry room and talk about how they used to save people. No wet feet allowed.

Religion and spirituality are synonyms for that deep human longing to experience the transcendent, to touch the divine. We all have this archetypal desire to translate or move the transcendent from its outer world formulation and make it into an intimate and immediate experience—meaning close to me. So if religion and spirituality are about trying to experience the holy, what are the opportunities or resources for that? One resource is the religious nature of the psyche, and how that religious nature has manifested itself in the history of the human enterprise through religion.

My colleagues, the evolutionary psychologists, will essentially reduce everything to a matter of survival, boiling it down to the idea that, "You can come up with all the theories you want about the collective and individual unconscious, symbols, myths, or whatever else, but the bottom line is, human beings are trying to survive. That's it. And they'll do whatever is necessary to survive, including believing in irrational 'miracles' and the illusionary concept of life after death."

These psychologists would concede that religion has perhaps served an evolutionary purpose by promoting values necessary for the survival of the species, such as love, compassion, nonviolence, and going forth and multiplying. At the same time, they say, if you take these God-fearing people of grace and back them into a corner, they'll do whatever it takes to survive, regardless of the religious instruction they have received.

I would agree with a lot of that, but I think there's much more to it. I agree that much of what constitutes religion has come into being to help us survive and to assuage ego anxiety. For example, humans seem to have an archetypal need to believe in a postgrave existence, and our myths have addressed this universal yearning with stories about how we can transcend our mortal limitations. More importantly, it seems to me that religion has entered into the human enterprise as a way to help us become more human, a task that is unique to our species. It's a vocation we should be very good at, but in reality it has been a very difficult and problematic assignment.

As I'm fond of saying, angels have no trouble being angels. Animals seem to have no trouble being animals. But humans are infamous in our inability to be human. Even dogs seem to get it just right, except when they're trying to act like humans. I've often cited the example of my little dog Kirby, God rest his soul. We found him on a Thanksgiving Day on Kirby Dr. in Houston, and like good Hebrew people, we named him for the site of his salvation.

When Kirby was being a loyal companion, barking when trouble was around, sniffing out things that might be threatening to his master, I would always say, "Good dog." But when he tried to eat at my table or sleep in my bed, I would say, "Bad dog." He wasn't being a bad human—he was just being a bad dog. He wasn't being true to his nature.

Likewise, we become inhuman when we act like animals instead of human beings. We don't seem to be able to always get it just right, as the animals do, except when they get mixed messages from us humans. (I often suspected Kirby's former owner had encouraged him to act like a human!) Skunks seem to be good at being skunks, and we human beings are also pretty good at being skunks. But often we're not very good at being human.

We often ask ourselves and each other, "Why did religion come into being?" and "What purpose does it serve?" I think the answer is that religion came into being to help us become better human beings.

If this is the answer, then why would we buy into a religion that denigrated the human enterprise? A religion that not only devalues our time here on earth as just preparation for something bigger and better to come, but one that also says to us from the very beginning, "You are bad." If we listen to John Calvin, father of the Puritan ethic, we're not simply bad but depraved, such miserable sinners that our only hope of salvation comes from a God who had to sacrifice his only son on our behalf. Think about that theology for a minute—does it make you feel better or worse? The guilt-inducing idea that Jesus died for our sins has even gotten into our theology, assuming all the authority normally reserved for scripturally based dogma. But like the idea of original sin, the concept of Christ dying for our sins is established nowhere in the Bible. Rather, it is theology that developed many years after Christ's death.

I'm much more interested in promoting a religion that values human beings and the human enterprise, rather than denigrating or devaluing them. Such a religion would fulfill the true promise of *religare*, to make us whole, to integrate us and put us back together. So much of the human condition is about being broken, being split off and separated from ourselves, that we desperately need the reconnecting salve of religion, so that we might truly find *salvo*, which means "to heal" and is the root word of *salvation*. Tragically, too much of religion has been about disintegration, exploiting and even creating all the guilt, shame, and complexes that keep us divided against ourselves.

Religion offers us some substantial resources for healing, integration, and wholeness, and two of the most vital resources are symbol and myth, which Campbell has called the song of the universe. The quandary for anyone seeking a fixed, absolute truth is that there have been thousands of symbols and myths throughout the history of humankind, and there have been just as many God images. I love that bumper sticker that shows symbols of the world's major religions, with the message that reads, "The Ways Are Many, The Light Is One." There, on one piece of vinyl, is the reality that we all seek the same light, the luminosity that archetypally has been associated with God. There are indeed many ways to God. I just happen to be a Christian, so for me the symbols and sacred stories of Christianity are my means of transport, but I have many fellow travelers all headed toward the same place I'm headed, using their own sacred stories and symbols to get there.

I wouldn't be surprised if the people who drive around with these enlightened bumper stickers—as few as they are—experience more than their fair share of traffic indignities. For a culture that is so obsessed with production and wealth, we don't view an abundance of religious expression as an asset. Instead, we are for the most part collectively stuck with an adolescent viewpoint that says, "Our truth is the only truth." That's an all-too-human response. Negative father exclusivity and reptilian territoriality are part of our human evolution, but that doesn't mean we can't outgrow that childish attitude.

Because we are so anxious, it is all too tempting to want to fix a concrete, never-changing, one-size-fits-all answer to that eternal question, "What is the truth?" We can describe truth in general terms. We can talk about what qualities it has and what it feels like, and one of those qualities is that truth is very elusive—too elusive, in fact, to define with any simplistic statement that goes something like, "The truth is…" I believe that truth and mystery are synonyms, and both are soul-nourishing fountains of living water, filled with wonder and amazement. Whatever it is, truth must ultimately be that ingredient that will empower and validate the human enterprise.

In addition to truth, we need religion to offer us a sense of meaning, and it does this through myths and symbols. If there has ever been a virgin birth anywhere, it would be the birth of our myths and symbols as they welled up out of the collective unconscious, or the world soul—pure and untainted by the intentions and pursuits of consciousness. In their purity, the myths and symbols are containers of content and information that can help us understand the human experience and approach transcendence. They do this through *Eros*, the connecting experience of the truth transmitted through our symbols and sacraments, and *Logos*, the word in the sense of the sacred story.

In the end, we are all after *it*. We need to understand and experience *it*. You can call *it* anything you choose, and we all know what we're talking about. We mean *God*. That's what we're after. If we were to be honest with ourselves, none of us truly understands either *it* or *God*, but that's what we all want. If I resonate with you, and we have a common experience of something transcendent, then I'm able to say to you, "You get it." We both know what the *it* is—it's the same as the Tao, that wellspring of Eastern religion that is generally translated as "the way."

In Taoism, they say, "Any Tao that you can understand is not the eternal Tao." In the Buddhist tradition, there is a wisdom that says, "If you see the Buddha on the road, run over him, because he is not the real Buddha." And in our Western tradition, the theologian Paul Tillich has said, "God is the God who appears when all of the other Gods disappear, in the anxiety of doubt." In other words, god is the ground of being that can't be comprehended. The God you comprehend is not God. We just can't get there.

Kimball suggests that we think of God or the transcendent as true north on the compass of each enduring religious tradition. He quotes Huston Smith from *Why Religion Matters:*

> The reality that excites and fulfills the soul's longing is God by whatsoever name. Because the human mind cannot come within light-years of comprehending God's nature, we do well to follow Rainer Marie Rilke's suggestion that we think of God as a direction rather than an object.[3]

God is ineffable, mysterious, and unknowable. The gods we have believed to be God throughout the millennia have been God images rather than God himself or herself. Our God images are the ways in which we have imagined God, and say more about us than they say about God. Thousands of dead gods litter the cosmic landscape, and each of these images was a time-bound constellation of the values and beliefs of the society that gave birth to the deity. As humans, we have long had the urge to create an anthropomorphic image of God, and it has been said that if horses had gods, their gods would look like horses.

Since the rise of the patriarchal monotheistic religions of Judaism, Christianity, and Islam, our God image has been that of a supernatural father figure in the sky, replacing earlier female God images that arose during matriarchal societies. For centuries, we have been playing out an often dysfunctional family drama in which we, the dependent children, do just about anything to please a stern celestial parent who is frequently capricious and cruel. We want our God to look over us and take care of us, and in our self-absorption and egocentricity we seldom stop to consider how we have limited—even crippled—our God images by projecting onto them our adolescent tribal mentalities.

As Spong points out, the ancient Jews had every reason to love their god Yahweh, but what about the many other tribes who were cruelly—and often unjustly—vanquished by this god? Were they not also children of God? Did they deserve their fates? The ancient Hebrews created a God in their own image, who shared their worldview, as innumerable tribes have done before and since.

Foremost, our God images came into being to help us answer the fundamental, narcissistic question of the child, which is, "Who is God? Is it I?" The role of the creation stories, in essence, is to set the record straight by establishing, "I am God and you are not." Of course, this clarification has not stopped many maniacal figures from proclaiming themselves to be God, but in general, the purpose of the creation story is so that we will worship God and not ourselves.

Once we give up on being God, then we can get about the enterprise of becoming human, which in itself is a pretty awesome task. Once we decide that this is a worthy task with life-affirming meaning and value, the first thing we need to do is give up on understanding God. We need to let that go. It's not going to happen, and the people who claim they understand God, or speak for God, scare me to death, for they have visited unspeakable physical and psychic pain upon this world. I don't have the statistics—I don't even believe it would be possible to get them—but I would not hesitate to state that if you added up all the evil and good deeds that have been committed in the name of God since humankind became conscious, the evil side of the ledger would far outbalance the good side. I don't think that's being cynical, but rather is realistic of the darkness of religion, as all the evidence from our centuries of inquisitions, witch hunts, genocides, and warfare would suggest.

To let go of understanding God, or speaking for God and divining his or her preferences and directives for our behavior, could be a major breakthrough in consciousness for the human species. I don't yet see it happening on any large scale, but one by one, we might be able to get there. Understanding God is within our experience, but it is beyond our comprehension. Most of the traditions I trust say, "Why don't you detach from the illusion that you're going to comprehend God?" We have many God images that we banter around in order to be able to talk about God, but they're not God.

After many years of pondering this myself, I have given up on understanding God. The farthest I can stretch it is to say that the Source of the mystery of the universe has allowed itself (or should I say himself, herself, themselves?) to be implanted into us as a resource. We just don't have the words to describe or speak about this ineffable mystery. Our comprehension is so limited, and our words are so imprecise. We try, but we just can't get there. As the Unitarian minister F. Forrester Church writes, "'God' is not God's name, but our name for that which is greater than all and yet present in each."

At my stage of development, the wisdom is giving up on this thing about understanding God and trying to focus now on understanding me. The theologian Clement of Alexandria said, "To know oneself is to know God," and I would add that some of the best resources for knowing ourselves are the myths and symbols of our religions.

The Divine Source is mysterious and unknowable, but it may be enough to know that this source has implanted itself in us, so that we each have some of this creator—or creatrix—within ourself as a resource for being human. Our purpose becomes not to try to understand God, but to understand what it means to be human, or as much as we can within the constraints of this time-bound ego and body we have been given.

If the purpose of religion is to help us become human, then myths and symbols are the resources we have for helping us accomplish this task. They are not resources for understanding God, but for understanding how humans have imagined God. This point is very important, and it is also very elusive, so please bear with me while I elaborate a bit.

The sacred stories we have are not about understanding God, but about understanding how we have imagined God through our God images. Foremost, this is what the Bible is about, a chronicle of the human imagination of God during one era and place in history, written by a bunch of late Iron Age desert scribes. If you were to sit down and read the Bible for yourself, instead of relying on an authority to interpret it for you, you would see that there are lots of different imaginations about God, even within this one single religious tradition. The Bible is filled with stories of different tribes, different voices, and different historical settings within the span of several thousand years.

The Bible is a library resource for understanding human beings. That's what the name means. We get *Bible* from *biblio*, the root word for "library." This is a very controversial and heretical statement to make in front of anyone who believes in the Bible as the literal word of God. I've said this before, and I've been strongly criticized. Centuries ago, I would have been burned at the stake. Even today, I may be kicked out of the church, excluded from polite company, but it's worth the risk for me.

Where did the content of the Bible come from, then? I believe it came up out of the collective unconscious. It's a beautiful dream that has been dreamt by my people, the Christian tribe. Now, that doesn't exclude God from the process, because who made the collective unconscious? If there is an imprint in the collective unconscious, who's the printer? But for my money, and for my understanding of Jung and depth psychology, the stories of the Bible (and all sacred texts and oral traditions) emerged out of the collective unconscious. Paradoxically, this doesn't make them any less valuable. It makes them much more valuable to us, because they reveal to us the nature of being human, which is the purpose of religion.

If religion is about the business of helping us to become human, then these sacred stories are about how to be human. That is what religion is. To me, the idea that these myths welled up out of the collective unconscious is a liberating and empowering realization. I get it now! What a relief!

With all my years in the church, I'm completely comfortable with the kind of pietistic language that says, "God inspired the Holy Scripture." I agree with that, because the inspiration came through the collective unconscious of human beings. In this archetypal structure, the truth resides in these containers called myths and symbols. So, God indeed works in mysterious ways—through us. I am much more comfortable with understanding the Bible in this way than I ever was thinking that Matthew, Mark, Luke, and John were simply automatons, transcribing revelations that came to them through auditory hallucinations. I feel a lot better with the idea that these scriptures emerged out of the human experience, that the authors of the gospels thought they were writing biography when in fact they were writing mythology, that they were vehicles for the collective unconscious of their community.

Despite my reputation as liberal, I am pretty conservative in one area. I think we all ought to read the Bible, or whatever resource contains the sacred text of our particular religion. We should read for ourselves, instead of relying on secondhand interpretations that might be intended to serve some interest other than your own.

You might be surprised that your experience with the stories may be far different from the first time you heard them, when somebody else interpreted them for you. These incredibly rich and varied stories are like diamonds that can be turned over and over, revealing different facets that can be appreciated in varied lights. They are like literary kaleidoscopes, so that when you turn them in different ways you can see different formations.

One of the most widely repeated stories of the Bible is the parable of the prodigal son, and it is even more valuable to us because scholars generally agree that the parables represent the most direct teachings handed down by Christ, without later figures such as St. Augustine and John Calvin doing the favor of interpreting for us.

The prodigal son is a wonderful example of what can happen when a son or daughter is empowered with their own authority. In this story, the prodigal son comes to his father one day and asks for his inheritance, which is given to him. The son goes off and squanders his inheritance on wine, women, and song. After he blows all his money, the misfortunes begin piling up, and he winds up working in a swine yard. His downward spiral of bad fortune continues, and it is not long before he finds himself down on his knees, eating the seedpods his boss has thrown out for the pigs. He had hit bottom, as they say in Alcoholics Anonymous. In AA, they describe the disease as a one-way elevator going down, which is a useful and accurate metaphor for any dark condition we find ourselves in. AA says we are free to get off the elevator at any floor, but in reality, most people just wait until they hit rock bottom and are forced to deal with their situation.

When the prodigal son hit bottom, "He came to himself," to quote a beautiful line of scripture. Which is to say, the prodigal son came to consciousness in that dark moment, when he realized he had squandered his inheritance and had not been true to himself. In that dark belly of the whale, surrounded by all the destruction and devastation he had created for himself and his family, he became conscious that he had misused his gift. Not only his financial gift, but the gift of life. After he came to himself, he returned home to his loving father, who embraced his son and forgave him, bestowing upon him the grace and blessing to begin a new life—a life in which he would be true to his Self.

It is often said that this parable could also be called the "Patient Father," which is appropriate because it takes a patient, supportive father—internal and/or external—to empower a son with the kind of autonomy that brings a prodigal son to make his own wise, life-affirming decision. If the prodigal son had had a negative, impatient father, the outcome of this parable would have undoubtedly been far different.

If we are to be conscious Bible readers, we need to develop a critical eye so that we may realize that of all the stories of the Bible, only a few are myths, which is to say only a few offer the kind of archetypal wisdom and transformative power that only myth can provide. Remember the definition from the little boy who was wise beyond his years: a myth isn't true on the outside, but it's true on the inside. And because a myth is archetypal in its content, it is true for all times and all places.

Most of the Bible is the history of one people, the Hebrew people of the Old Testament and the emerging Christian tribe of the New Testament. Much of the Bible is what the Germans call *Heilsgeschichte*, or sacred history, but it is history nonetheless.

We can now get a little critical and say, "Well this is more about the history of the Hebrew people than it is about God, although there are some very helpful myths in here." (Including one myth that has reshaped the world, which we'll get to in the next chapters.) We can continue: "Inasmuch as the Bible is about God, it is really about the God images of this tribe, and how they evolved over the centuries." We can see that the myths are pure representations of the eternal, timeless archetypes, which take shape in containers with content that informs us about what it means to be human.

Another benefit of reading the Bible is that you also begin to see what is *not* in it. Most pew-sitting Christians believe the concept of original sin is contained in the Bible and therefore is the inerrant word of God. Whether one prefers a literal reading of the Bible or not, original sin is not to be found anywhere in the New or Old Testament. Rather, this idea was St. Augustine's interpretation of the creation myth, formulated several centuries after Christ lived.

All theology is autobiography, and much of St. Augustine's drive to purge Christianity of its feminine qualities, especially any hint of instinctuality, had much to do with his own struggle with his mother complex. So this Augustinian version of Christianity, which most of us grew up with, has within it the idea that we are flawed from the beginning, and that instinctuality is bad and must be repressed.

There are all kinds of assumptions like this that we could explore. We could question Saint Paul, for example. What if he was wrong? What if he misinterpreted what Jesus was saying? The idea that Saint Paul's theology was autobiographical is a scary thought for many Christians, because for most of their lives they have assumed that what Saint Paul said was what God said. I don't think St. Paul was wrong in his larger interpretation, but I would disagree with some of the particularities and peculiarities of his teachings, such as his cultural viewpoints about women and human sexuality.

The Bible tells a long, interesting narrative of human development and how our God image has developed along with us. The essence of our religion is in the sacred story, in the word, not in the institution. The word is our attempt to try to understand and make reason out of the human experience, and to do so in a healthy way. The institutional church came into being to serve as a caretaker for the word, charged with the responsibility for keeping it alive. I was ordained in the Episcopal Church, and in our tradition, the bishop gives the new priest a Bible and a chalice, which I always interpreted as, "Keep the story alive and keep the mystery present."

One of the most helpful and redeeming messages the sacred stories tell us is that we can't live our lives without making mistakes. We can't do it without difficulties and losses. In every one of the sacred stories, the heroes and heroines are fools and cheaters. They are murderers, like Moses, and adulterers, like David. In other words, they are human just like us.

The stories contain these archetypal themes of the human experience, along with the hopeful message that we can persevere in spite of our limited knowledge and freedom, that we make mistakes and have losses, but that there is something in the cosmos that can redeem our human failings and limitations. There is a force that uses our way of fumbling through life for growth and evolution, for a kind of richness or prosperity that can only come from a consciousness that embraces the nonmaterial and the nonrational.

Could it be that this archetypal energy could have as its purpose healing in the here and now? The exploitation of the idea would be using it for reward and punishment: "If you're a good girl, you'll get to go there, and if you're a bad girl, you'll have to go there."

That is exploitation, punitiveness. But maybe there's a healing aspect to the experience for now, out of the archetypal idea of eternity. I would agree with that. That if one really, truly lives in the present, then time and space both disappear. There's not past and future. It's just the eternal now.

I said to a man I've worked with for years (he's a wonderful guy, but a little too logical for me): "What prevents you from living in the present?" He said, "Well the past and the future." It is very difficult to live in the present.

I do believe that this time-limited experience, the birth we didn't request and the grave we can't escape, has meaning and purpose for the here and now. There's something more than mere survival going on here, and I think part of faith is giving ourselves to something we don't fully understand.

I can only explain my experience of God, and the myths are resources for helping me to understand how my people, the Christian tribe, have experienced the transcendent nature of God, and how they have created sacred stories, images, and symbols out of this experience. If the function of religion is to help us become whole, the biblical stories, myths, and symbols that came up out of the collective unconscious are the resources for the human enterprise of healing and health. That's what they're there for.

Word and sacrament. Logos and Eros. Myth and symbol. These are the essence of what religion is about, which is to help us become human. These resources must be kept alive and available to us, and every generation has to critique the custodians of those symbols in order to maintain their life force and vitality. That's our job. We have to do that! We must do that!

Many conservatives and fundamentalists refer to people like me as revisionists, and I'm complimented by that, because I think the stories need to be revised. They need to be seen and heard again with critical eyes and ears in the twenty-first century. We keep the stories alive when we interpret them for ourselves and ask questions about their relevance to our own lives. As it says in Proverbs, without vision, the people perish.

We place our religious resources in grave danger when we rely on so-called religious authorities to do the interpreting for us. The myths of the Bible, such as the creation myth of Adam and Eve, came out of the collective unconscious, and the male authorities of a very patriarchal culture edited the Bible, canonized it, and interpreted it for us. The men were put in charge of the myths, and they messed them up. That's why I recommend that we read the Bible for ourselves and become our own authorities.

I understand the reliance on religious authorities, especially in our time-crunched and complex modern world. We can't know all there is to know about everything. I know next to nothing about cars, for example, and I don't do all the due diligence I should on understanding how my car works and knowing how to tell a good, honest mechanic from a rotten one. God knows I have been exploited through the years by the automotive authorities I have relied on.

We also need to be careful who we take our cars to, vis-à-vis religion. Very few of us have time to do the theology and study the scriptures and classic texts for ourselves, so we look to the authorities to tell us what's going on under the hood. Even on those many occasions that the myth does get perverted by an authority, maybe even a well-meaning authority who in 90 percent of his interpretation was helpful, all we remember is the 10 percent that wasn't helpful, and that may add to our feeling of being religiously wounded or exiled.

For some, questioning the purported inerrancy of the Bible is heretical. For others, it's liberating. I say take whatever train that will get you where you need to go, but for me, I want to be on a liberation train, which for me means to become my own authority, granting myself the right to critique the self-appointed religious authorities and power brokers. That's where the opportunity for growth is. A large part of the human enterprise is for us to eventually, sometime in our lives, stand up and say, "I am ready to live my life. I'm going to become my authority and act as the interpreting body for my own life. That's my responsibility—and privilege—and I can't or won't abdicate it to an external authority."

Claiming our autonomy and authority is the most exhilarating part of the human enterprise, and it's something we must do, despite the cost. And the cost is often dear, but the cost of not doing so is even greater, for we deny ourselves entry into the kingdom of God.

My own journey was that I finally woke up one day and said, "I'm going to quit being afraid of this and quit avoiding it. I'm going to get myself to it. I want to get in it and live it. I may make mistakes and I may be criticized, and there will be those who don't like the way I'm doing it, but I'm going to do it."

This is what's commonly called a conversion experience, and when it comes in the form of claiming rather than abdicating authority, of deciding to seek truth and mystery at whatever cost, rather than trying to desperately fix the truth to a dead God image, then it is truly a liberating and life-affirming experience. It was a nonlinear rather than linear process that led me to the point where I finally could say, "I'm going to live my life."

I can't tell you the exact time and date it happened for me, but I can tell you when my journey began. On my 30th birthday, I was a parish priest in Kansas City, and a group of friends and parishioners gifted me with a set of Jung's *The Collected Works*, a 20-volume set that was an amazingly generous and thoughtful gift. I had been fascinated by Jung's psychology ever since I first read *The Undiscovered Self* in seminary. That afternoon, as I sat down in my study to acquaint myself with the books, I had one of those sublime synchronistic[4] moments, when I opened a volume at random, and my eyes fell upon a verse that would set my theology and psychology off in a new direction for the rest of my life. It was Volume 11 of *The Collected Works*, in which Jung writes:

Are we to understand the "imitation of Christ" in the sense that we should copy his life and, if I may use the expression, ape his stigmata; or in the deeper sense that we are to live our own proper lives as truly as he lived his in its individual uniqueness? It is no easy matter to live a life that is modeled on Christ's, but it is unspeakably harder to live one's own life as truly as Christ lived his.[5]

It was Jung's Christology that helped me to realize that on Judgment Day—wherever and whatever that means—God would not say to me, "Pittman, why are you not like Christ?" Instead, God would ask, "Pittman, why are you not like Pittman?"

Even after that breakthrough, living life as my own authority has still not been a linear process. I still have days when I don't want my life, when I want to turn it over to God or let Jesus live it for me. There are still times when I want to go back to being five or six, so I could look to someone to tell me what to do. God knows I've had my regressive moments, and I reserve the right to have them for the rest of my life, because that's part of being human.

But in the main, in my best moments, I will only take responsibility for living the paradox and remaining in the present. I'm not going to wait. I'm not going to waste this precious life just getting prepared for something that might or might not come later. And if I'm wrong and the God of the Bible is the literal God, is he going to punish me for living my life abundantly? I'll take the risk of going to hell, wherever and whatever that might be.

## CHAPTER 6

# CHRISTIANITY'S SYMBOLS AND SACRED STORIES

The most basic definition we can formulate for any religion is that it is a set of symbols and sacred stories that the caretakers of the faith try to keep alive.

Symbols are the jewels that Eve smuggled out of Eden, numinous and transcendent, pointing beyond themselves to truths and mysteries. We humans are a symbol-making species. We have a nonrational need to experience the transcendent, and symbols are our nonrational media for getting to that place. The word *symbol* is a compound of *bol*, which comes from *bolon* and means "to throw," and *sym*, which means "with." So the most basic meaning of symbol—"to throw you with"—speaks of the dynamic emotional movement offered by a symbol.

Symbols are not to be confused with signs, which simply point to rational, material facts, such as the speed limit or a curved road ahead. A symbol, on the other hand, points beyond itself to that which is mysterious, transrational, and nonmaterial. If a plane is the only vehicle that can transport us at a certain altitude and velocity, then a symbol is the only vehicle that can take us to the realm of the transcendent.

The sacred stories, or myths, carry the ancient archetypes and allow us to see the transcendent at work in the world. With help from the contributions of Jung and Campbell, the postmodern world has revitalized myth as a substantial and reverent word, which far from attempting to trivialize a story as make-believe, recognizes the timeless and eternal truths carried within it. To our benefit, we have reclaimed the idea of myth as a vehicle through which the transcendent can be experienced.

My colleague Hollis writes in his book *Mythologems:*

> Myth is perhaps the most important psychological and cultural construct of our time. In a culture committed to the world of matter, access to the invisible world—which myth makes possible, along with its two chief instruments, metaphor and symbol—has never been more critical in allowing some balance of the spirit.[1]

Every religion has such a set of symbols and sacred stories, representing the wisdom of the tribe and the eons of experience illuminating how this religious family has pursued the human enterprise in a healthy manner.

In this chapter, I'm going to attempt to analyze the symbols and stories of Christianity, because this is the tribe I belong to, and I'm a shaman of this tribe. But we could easily do the same thing for the symbols and stories of Islam, Buddhism, or Hinduism, for the resources of these religions have been equally efficacious for their followers, and in some respects have been more successful than Christianity in pursuing some aspects of humanity, such as the Buddhist knack for being mindful and present. To claim that the symbols and stories of Christianity are the only ones that have efficacy would be straying into the darkness of negative father exclusivity.

Whatever religion we talk about, let's not focus on following the rules of that particular culture in order to gain reward and avoid punishment in the sweet hereafter. That would be the real trivializing of a powerful resource for living. As a Jungian, I'm far more interested in looking at religion as a psychotherapeutic system. This is not to say that the chief essence of religion is psychological rather than theological, but religion does have significant psychological implications for healing.

If we were to weave a tapestry of Christianity, we could start by building a loom and putting in it the four threads that are essential to the faith. These four threads include the symbols of baptism and the Eucharist, which stand out as most important in the Christian tradition because they are the ones that the founder of the faith asked us to continue. Then there are the sacred stories of Christmas and Easter, with their beautiful messages about incarnation and resurrection, providing the bookends for the Christian myth.

With these four elements, we can begin to create a framework for a truly living religious tradition, rather than the dead traditionalism so many of us have come to associate with religion. The difference between tradition and traditionalism is that the latter is the dead faith of the living. The former, however, is the living faith of the dead, which has been passed down to us so that we may have these resources to experience God in our present lives. That is why it is such an awesome responsibility for us to keep the symbols and sacred stories alive, and in some cases to bring them back from the dead, not only for ourselves but for future generations.

The liberal religious educator Angus MacLean said that we should not be content to be the mere "bellhops of history, passing the baggage of one generation on to another." He said we have to unpack the baggage and make it our own, not worshipping history and culture like hidebound fetishes or dead idols, but "to feed them into our living, creative stream of personal life for spiritual and intellectual reprocessing."[2] Amen, I say, and let us begin unpacking.

## BAPTISM

Jesus said at the first supper, "Do this in remembrance of me." He also said, "I want you to baptize. Go into all the world and baptize in the name of the Father and the Son, and the Holy Spirit." It's interesting that the trinity formula hadn't developed when he was speaking, but let's give some credit to the possibility that some redaction might have gone on.

Let's look at this initiatory symbol called baptism in a larger sense, outside of the narrow box of Christian theology. As prolific symbol makers, we humans have always tended to use the natural elements, such as earth and trees, moon and stars, sky and fire, for our symbols. The symbolism of baptism is about the most elementary element of them all: water.

Water, archetypally, has always been a symbol for mother and the maternal. We come out of the amniotic fluid of the water of our gestation. In the evolutionary process, all of creation was birthed out of water.

In the mythical story of creation, God moved water over dust to make clay, and then he animated the clay by breathing life into it. I much prefer this mythological account of creation to Darwin's theory of how our most remote predecessors evolved out of the primordial muck. Darwin's theory may be the scientific truth, and I can have that along with the Genesis story, which is much more poetic and gets to the spiritual truth of our creation. With the right viewpoint, we can have our cake and eat it too, and we can lead much fuller, richer, and more meaningful lives in the process. We can have science and symbolism, the rational and the nonrational, inner and outer truth.

Water has many efficacious functions for us. It's a cleaning element, as well as an agent for healing and sustenance. We thirst and water sustains us. Without it we would die. Water is not only that out of which we were born, but is that which continues to feed us, nurture us, and give us life.

I'm not a big cat fan, but I like all kinds of metaphors, and I love to watch a mother cat clean her baby. It's a beautiful thing to watch. When I was a boy, my mother used to spit on a rag and clean my face when it was dirty and wash up my knees when they were scraped. Despite all our material breakthroughs, water is still probably the best healing and cleaning element we have. It is certainly the element from which all others are derived.

Water is also soothing. Our first experience was of water as a shock absorber when we floated around in the womb. And for most of us when we are angry, tired, lonely, or sick, what provides the greatest comfort? To just take a hot bath or a long shower.

Seventy percent of our body is water, and we water in all kinds of important transitions. We perspire, we cry, we urinate. When something important is happening, human beings are watering. It is a constant part of the human experience. It's interesting to me too, that the Spanish word for sea, derived from the Latin, is *mar*. Mar is sea, and our mother is Mary. Can we see the connection?

We have a strong mother association with water. We emerged from the amniotic fluid when our mother's water broke. On a mythical level, we became one with the water of creation when God moved over the dust with water and made us. We've come through the Red Sea, and we've come through the Jordan River and the flood. This passing through water has been going on for a long time in our tradition.

When Jesus came along, it was a custom to proselytize non-Jews with a bathing ritual, because the Jews were very big on dietary laws and cleanliness. And so it was a symbolic rite when you were a proselyte and you wanted to become a Jew. You had to take a bath.

John did that with Jesus. He baptized Jesus as a symbol of a new life, creating a wonderful mythological story about a different kind of birth that is available to us. We can talk about what kind of birth it is, but at the very least, it's a birth into a new kind of consciousness. As a symbolic process, baptism is an outward visible sign of something that goes on inside us, which is a transformation from living just in the kingdom of the world into living in the kingdom of God. It symbolizes living with a higher kind of consciousness than simply biological reaction and survival.

So Jesus said, "From now on, go wash people and let that be a symbol of them being re-born into the kingdom of God." What a wonderful ritual process with efficacious meaning, using the deep archetypal energy of mother water!

As is so typical with institutional life, the sacrament of baptism evolved, and soon everybody got into fights over when and how and whom you baptize. We've argued over infant baptism, believer's baptism, whether you use water, whether you sprinkle or immerse, and so forth. It is part of our human nature to take something that is sacred and trivialize it. Our saving grace is that we also have the ability to raise everyday objects from our quotidian lives to the level of symbol and sacrament.

This idea of creating a tradition where we use water and having a public ceremony where the person to be baptized assents to being born again into a new consciousness, an awareness of another world that exists within this one. It is such a beautiful and efficacious ritual. I wish we would just do it and not interpret it so much, much less argue about the trivial details. Here I am interpreting it myself, but in a way, I wish we would just do it and let everybody kind of figure it out on their own. Sacramental activity provides contact with the unconsciousness, and the term *ex opere operato* refers to the more or less automatic effectiveness of the sacrament, whether we are conscious of the symbolism or not.

There's an energy process something going on in the baptismal ritual that is more than human, even while it is fairly transparent. The myth tells us that God took the clay and moved the mist over it, blowing the spirit into it, animating and ensouling it to become a human being. We enact that same process of the baptism sacrament. We take a human being, whether a baby or an adult, and we take the dust that we are and we put water onto it, and then we invoke the spirit and boom! They are animated into a new consciousness, a new life, a new sense of being, whether they're aware of it or not.

Baptism is not the kind of initiation that you outgrow. Baptism is a kind of initiation into which you grow. I don't suspect that any of us has really fully understood or grown into our baptism. We outgrow most kinds of initiations, such as our initiations into fraternities, sororities, and lodges. But baptism is initiation we are continuously growing into. I can tell you that I still ponder the efficacy of my own baptism and how it continues to transform me.

We've put a lot of baggage on baptism, like forgiveness of sins, for instance. I'm not as interested in having my sins forgiven as I am having my consciousness changed about what sins are, because our association of what constitutes a sin is just another part of that negative father archetype that is trying to make and enforce the rules.

Jungian psychology has implications for theology, the primary one being that Jung believed that there really is an incarnation, that God is present within each of us. To truly understand baptism is to get a sense of depth and breath of this significant thing that has been trivialized into "your ticket to heaven." Baptism is not a ticket into heaven, but a ticket into a way to be in this world that is meaningful and healthy. That's what the good father and mother do for the child. They nurture the child and empower her to live into the world in a way that is meaningful, healthy, and abundant, rather than a way that is shameful and limited by fear and infantilism.

Baptism is a symbol with efficacious implications for the human enterprise, but only if it does not become a dead symbol. In England, they talk about "let's do the child." When the attitude is a perfunctory, "We are going to go do the baby," then baptism has probably become an empty ritual, a broken image that has lost its life.

To keep baptism alive, the great commission is that we should go forth and baptize everybody in the world. If we took that commission seriously, what would it look like, and how would we act? I think our mission would be to help people all over the world discover the kingdom of God and hear the message of the Gospel using the symbols, sacred stories, and ritual processes available to them in their indigenous cultures. If we helped them attain what we seek through our faith, but using their own resources, then we would have for the first time created a truly catholic or universal faith. As a people helper, I'm not interested in making people Christian, but I'm interested in making them holy.

## EUCHARIST

In all the profundity of sacramental theology, essentially the church offers us two things: a bath and a meal. The former is baptism, the latter is the Eucharist. Far from being meager rations, these offerings are abundant, even empowering, for they give us energy and strength for our spiritual journey. What else would somebody need on a journey, except a bath and a meal? It's very simple while at the same time very profound.

When my brother and I were growing up in the little town of Drumright, Oklahoma, we spent every day outside, rain or shine. At the end of the day, my mother would stand on the front porch and call out, "Come in, boys. It's time to wash up and eat." Baptism and Eucharist, right? Eating is very important, is it not? More than important, it is necessary for survival. Just as a mother feeds her child, here is the mother church offering a meal.

The people of God, or just the people, have always exhibited this drive to elevate our most basic activities into sacred rituals. We elevate our instinctive attraction to water into baptism and thus make it a vehicle for achieving a higher consciousness. With the Eucharist, we take the meal ritual and raise it up to the status of sacrament. We've been doing meal rituals as long as we've been eating, and the wisdom of both Jesus and the church was to take something we did every day, at least once a day, and the raise the profane, mundane, quotidian ritual called eating into a sacrament.

Since we are all going to be doing it all the time, why don't we use it for a symbol? We are going to be bathing all the time. Why don't we use that for a symbol? Very wise!

We all have our own meal rituals. I mean there are two kinds of eating. There is the re-fueling, and there's the dining. And dining generally doesn't have to do with hunger. It has to do with the ability to relate and have human intercourse around this eating, and to make it a ritual. If we want to be with somebody we know or want to get to know somebody, we ask them to dine with us. And it's really not about eating. It's about having a meeting of hearts and minds. As the novelist James Salter has said, "The meal is the essential act of life…the habitual ceremony." As Johnson says, the simplest meal is worth remembering for a lifetime if it is the carrier of human meaning and connection.

There was a meal ritual in Judaism, and it was fairly simple. The father or the leader of the tribe would always bless the wine or the drink and the bread or the food. Jesus, being the rabbi for his group, performed the meal ritual. As the rabbi at the table, he said, "From now on, when you do this, do it in remembrance of me," using the Greek translation *anamnesis* for the word *remembrance*.

The meaning of *anamnesis* is subtly yet significantly different than our own definition of remembrance, which has to do with recalling something that happened in the past. *Anamnesis* gets to the ritual of re-membering, which like *re-ligio* has to do with putting back together that which has been dis-membered. In this sense, that which is being remembered is present. It is among us. Essentially, Jesus said, "I will be present in the meal." He was saying that he would be present every time in the future, when we blessed the bread and the wine and dined together.

*Incarnation* means "to come in flesh." Jesus said to his disciples, "This is my flesh, and this is my blood. And from now on, when you do this, do it in re-membrance of me." So, we can see that the incarnation of Christ is present in the Eucharist and in every meal, if we call his presence into consciousness.

In the Episcopal tradition, when the priest is preparing the elements for the Eucharist, there is some important symbolic action taking place at the altar, where the priest takes a little water and puts it in the wine. This is not to lessen the effect of the wine, but to symbolize the water of the amniotic fluid, the water of the Red Sea and the Jordan River. It's the water of baptism and creation. The priest takes the body, puts the water in the wine, invokes the Holy Spirit, and animates those elements.

The sacrament transports the archetypes into the present its symbols, which carry transformative powers for those who have the eyes to see and the ears to hear. Like I said earlier, it is ingenious of the human creative ability to take these trivial things and make them sacred. Part of consciousness raising is to try to realize that we are taking the mundane and looking at it as miraculous, and taking the ordinary and looking at it as extraordinary.

We used to teach in Sunday school that when you put the candles out in church, it doesn't mean that the light—which symbolizes the presence of God—disappears, but rather that the light goes everywhere. Likewise, the sacramental principle of the Eucharist is that God is present in the bread and wine. That's not making these elements into idols, but simply saying that the bread and wine symbolize that God is present everywhere, even in our most mundane and simple activities. The Eucharist reminds us that any time people eat together in a conscious desire to meet, there is an incarnation of love, or an incarnation of the presence of the Creator and the created who are connecting with one another.

There's an old saying that when you go to the well, the amount of water you get is dependent on the size of your bucket. So if you go to the well of the sacraments with a small, narrow understanding, that's what you get. But if you go with a bigger understanding, so that the efficacy of the symbol is in the participant, not in the symbol, you can drink deeply. I don't think the ritual makes as much difference as what's going on inside the person and how much energy and consciousness we are able to project onto the symbol.

## CHRISTMAS

Now that we've looked at the symbols of Christianity, what about the stories? We could start by analyzing the Christmas and Easter stories, those bookends of the Christian myth that tell us of a miraculous birth and an equally miraculous rebirth. As the Unitarian minister John Buehrens notes, these holidays "remind us to find the mark of God less in the irregularities of nature than in the unexpected turns that life can take, in the humbling of the arrogant and the uplifting of the lowly."[3]

The message of Christmas is unconditional love, shown in one of its many facets by the example of Joseph, who stood by the side of his unexpectedly pregnant bride. Delving even deeper, the essence of the Christmas story is incarnation, the very idea that there would be within the human being something of the divine, that we could experience the mystery, the wonder, and, yes, the love of God in our own bodies, and that within the human experience lies the possibility of existing in unity with all other creatures and organisms.

Christmas is a story about mother, about birthing, about the idea of God becoming incarnate and coming into the world in a conscious way. In celebrating the Christmas story, we say that we are going to be conscious that God is in the world, that God has come into the world in the form of a human being. This idea is very consistent with Christian theology, although Christianity has not had a very strong emphasis on the divinity of the human being. We have had much emphasis on the dark, weak, and evil aspects of being human, with hardly any focus on our divine nature.

The idea that God could be fully present in one human being would be pretty heretical for Judaism. This religion would not disagree with the notion that people have been inspired by God, but for a human being to actually *be* God, that would be pretty blasphemous. What would be even more blasphemous would be for us to take this idea seriously, but there's little danger in that, because nobody seems to have yet taken seriously that idea that God could be incarnated in human beings.

Let me go back to the sacramental principal for anyone who might be looking for the logic of this analysis. In the sacramental tradition, you set something aside as sacred, which is not to say that the sacredness is located in that object, but rather that the object is a symbol that sacredness is everywhere. If the story tells us that God is incarnated in one human being, it does so to illustrate that God is incarnated in every human being! That's what the incarnation is about. There is a God within each of us. Christ dwells within each of us.

The Christmas story, reclaimed from all the commercializing and sentimentalizing that has had the effect of trivializing it, is about the radical idea that God would enter history through a human being born of a human mother (who by the way has been sentimentalized right out of her humanity). This story—telling us that we have within us something of the divine, that a divine spark is available to us for healing, transformation, and consciousness—seems to me to be efficacious in the human enterprise.

Most of us look forward to Christmas every year, but we need to remind ourselves that the incarnation is continuing. We don't have to wait until December 25 to celebrate a one-time incarnation that happened over 2,000 years ago. Incarnation can take place every day, every moment. When we baptize, we are saying that the incarnation is continuing in this person. We have dust and water, then the breath of God animates, breathing life and spirit into the soul being baptized. Thus we have incarnation—Christmas is in every baptism.

## EASTER

Easter, of course, is the resurrection story, a dramatic reminder that new life is available to us at any time, even in the midst of what seems to be the most disintegrating time imaginable. The symbolism informs us that, if we have a consciousness of incarnation as an ongoing possibility, we can be reborn or resurrected at any time, just as Christ was.

Resurrection is about existential change, not just about postgrave change. We can see that the human experience is about resurrectional power and transformation, so that death can be transformed into new life at any time. We have many deaths in our lives—the deaths of old attitudes and ways of being in the world—and to have a resurrectional consciousness available to us during our journey is a great gift offered by Christianity. The contribution that the Easter story makes to consciousness is to help us recognize that there is no Easter without Good Friday.

What psychologists call dis-membering is important for re-membering. So the breaking apart or fracturing is an important part of the next stage of evolution. It is an important part of the "logic" of the sacrifice.

In the Jungian viewpoint, Jesus is to God what the ego is to Self, symbolizing the dismemberment or crucifixion that the ego has to experience to get to one's ultimate stage of development, where the Self reigns supreme. Symbolically, crucifixion is the letting go of all the attachments we have made, those material things we cling to that only offer false hope and temporary distraction. We have to let all that go if we are to get to the next stage of development, where each of us can become our authentic Self, following the model of Christ.

It is important to distinguish between resurrection and resuscitation. When Jesus brought Lazarus back from the dead, that was resuscitation. And in our own lives, we seek to resuscitate our marriages, careers, relationships, and ideas by trying to breathe new life into them, rather than letting them die or stay dead. Death, final and accepted, is a requirement for resurrection, which brings a completely new life into being where there was none before. Our old attitudes won't work in the new life, the new consciousness. So if we truly want resurrection, we must be careful not to settle for resuscitation.

## CHAPTER 7

# THE KINGDOM WITHIN

In the late 1950s, when the Soviet *Sputnik* became the first manned space-craft to journey into outer space, one cosmonaut reported a startling discovery: "I have been up into the heavens, and God is not there."

Well, of course not. "Up into the heavens" was never where God was, no matter how strong our urge to project our God image onto a supernatural father figure in the sky. No subsequent astronaut has found God in outer space, and none ever will, because the kingdom of heaven is not up in the skies, but in a place much more intimate and immediate for each human being.

Before I go any further, I want to note that this chapter is based on a course I taught at the Jung Center of Houston in 2006, called "The Kingdom Within." I chose the title and topic as a tribute to my dear friend, the Jungian analyst and Episcopal priest John Sanford, who died in 2005. Sanford's seminal book, also titled *The Kingdom Within*, had just reached the 25-year mark since its first publication. His thesis that the kingdom of God is not a supernatural, extraterrestrial concept, but rather a state of consciousness and a way of being in the world that is accessible to all of us, has never felt more resonant with myself and other members of the religious exile community seeking the living water of a healthy spirituality for the twenty-first century.

I agree with Sanford that one of the best and highest functions of religion is its efficacy as a psychotherapeutic system, with tremendous potential to bring about healing, wholeness, and inner peace and well-being. In fact, this may be religion's most valuable contribution to human existence and to our continued survival as a species, for we can only change the world and our relationships with others after we change ourselves from within. In this chapter, I use the *kingdom of God*, the *kingdom of heaven*, and the *kingdom within* all as synonyms for the same basic premise, the idea that when Jesus and others talked of this kingdom, they were referring to an inner world and symbolic realm for each person, as opposed to a concrete, exterior reality.

## CHRIST AS A SYMBOL OF SELF

We begin with the idea that the kingdom of God is archetypal, for this concept has been present in many forms, in many tribes and cultures throughout history. Thus, it is universal, transpersonal, and valid in every place and time. It may not be true on the outside, but it is true on the inside.

Another foundation of the kingdom within is that Christ is a symbol of the Self, and this also appears to be archetypal, for many cultures have developed collective myths about manna personalities—*manna* meaning anything badly needed that comes unexpectedly, like a savior. In each myth, the community projects the symbol of the Self onto the manna personality, who constellates and carries that projection. Like similar projections we make onto parental and romantic figures, most projections of the Self eventually fail or wear out, because the object of our projection isn't strong or enduring enough to carry our unconscious desires. Religious history is strewn with dead manna personalities, and it is a tremendous testament to Christ that his myth has been able to carry this projection in so many different centuries and cultures.

The best thing we can do for the object of any projection—be it a projection of mother, father, love, or Self—is to pull back the projection and remove the burden from the object, while still remaining open to the energy that is available from the archetype. The best thing you can do for Jesus is to follow his example and become yourself as authentically as he became himself, regardless of the cost or sacrifice asked of you. That's what Jesus taught, and that's why he constellated a projection of the Self for his tribe, and why that community created an enduring, life-sustaining myth around him.

One of our deepest archetypal longings is the psyche's drive toward wholeness, and Jesus represented for his followers the ability to live a healthy, balanced, and integrated life, with equal access to one's masculine and feminine archetypal energy, regardless of one's own gender. When it was time to be masculine, he was masculine, taking on the Pharisees and laying out hard spiritual truths with no sentimentality. When it was time to be feminine, he was feminine, healing the sick and offering emotional comfort. Sometimes Christ was loving and confirming and related, and at other times he was sharp as a sword. He would withdraw in an introverted way, which is an archetypally feminine way of being, or he could be with the crowds in an extraverted way, an archetypally masculine trait. He could be logical and sensate, or feeling and intuitive.

Christ was not always consistent in his actions and attitudes, but he was consistently appropriate. Life does not call us to be consistent, for circumstances are ever-changing. So similar to what the Buddhists call living mindfully, the kingdom of God is a way of knowing how to respond appropriately to whatever situation we find ourselves in. We are able to do this because we are conscious, living in the present moment, and we have access to the masculine and feminine totality of our psyche, having integrated into consciousness those parts formerly split off or repressed as shadow material. When it is time to be called into a maternal matrix of consciousness, then we are able to summon forth our ability to be accommodating, containing, and feeling toward ourselves and others. When it's appropriate to be definitive, discerning, and assertive, then we are called to act out of our masculine archetypal energy. Christ modeled how, rather than mix the masculine and feminine archetypes together into some inferior form of each, we must hold them together consciously, as opposites, so that we can do as he did and draw from the pure energy of each archetype at the appropriate time.

That's what the myth says about Jesus, and it mirrors back to us the nature of what the Self is. Through the Christian myth, we can begin to see Jesus as a representation—a *re-presentation*—of the possibility of achieving authentic human Selfhood. For reasons both mysterious and mystical—which satisfies the first of the four functions of myth as identified by Campbell—Christ constellated the potential of Selfhood for this community in Jerusalem, and they projected onto him the archetype of the Self.

Siddhartha did that in another community in another time, and he became known as the Buddha. Part of the myth of Hinduism is that Atman is the indwelling of the holy, as contrasted to the extraverted nature of the Brahma. We can begin to see that the projection is archetypal because it occurs at different places at different times, but regardless of whether we're talking about Jesus, Siddhartha, or Atman, it's the same archetype of the Self being projected out from different communities onto different figures at different times. Whether Jesus Christ the man, the mortal time-limited human being, actually did what the myth tells us is irrelevant. What is relevant is what his myth has to say to me. This makes it absolutely vital to me that Jesus of Nazareth was a human being, because if he wasn't then his myth really doesn't have anything to say to me.

What exactly is the Self? Jung developed this term to describe the essence and totality of the human psyche, and he also often used it as a synonym for God. Paradoxically, the Self is the center of the psyche, and at the same time, it is the circumference. It is simultaneously both the inward nature of who I am, and the sum of all that I am.

The Self is the force that holds all of the psyche's disparate, paradoxical, and often conflictual elements together. The Self integrates rather than disintegrates; it creates rather than destroys. It is the part of the psyche that generates and transforms life. It is that aspect of ourselves that urges—even requires—us to continue to evolve as we muddle along in our journey to wholeness. The Self will lead us to the bliss that Campbell urged us to follow. To be human is to have a Self, but to be estranged, alienated, or disconnected from this Self is to suffer tremendously.

Developing the Self is synonymous with the idea of *individuation,* another term coined by Jung. Individuation refers to the process in which our undifferentiated characteristics are developed and integrated into an indivisible whole, so that we become our authentic selves, just as Christ became his authentic self. In order to individuate, the ego—that provisional self-image we create and cling to for conformity and approval—must be subordinated to the true nature of the Self.

Individuation is what John was talking about when he said, "I must decrease and He must increase." That is the proper relation of ego to Self, especially in the second half of life, when the Self is called to take authority. This journey can begin by asking, "What is it that I am called to be in this time and space, rather than that which I was told I must conform and adapt to?" Adaptation and conformity are survival techniques for the first half of life, and shouldn't be judged, because the Self is naturally undeveloped and immature, and the anxious ego simply wants to survive. But for the second half of life, authenticity is necessary for survival. When the voice of the Self speaks, it's about truth, contrasted to the ego's pleas for security and conformity. If the call to Selfhood is not honored, the Self will do whatever it needs to do to get our attention, which is why the so-called midlife crisis is pervasive in our largely unconscious society.

In the kingdom of God, we are called upon to integrate that part of us that is the ego's opposite, the shadow. The shadow contains those things we find intolerable about ourselves, and rather than be conscious of our shadow material, we project it onto other people, who in almost every case are members of minority groups. One of the things we see in adolescent development is that ego wants to be in the in-group, and one of the ways we do that is by putting down the out-group, whatever minority group is most convenient at the time to project our repressed and inferior feelings onto.

If we are to be worthy of the kingdom of God, we must become conscious of our shadows and let go of our territorialism and judgments about the perceived inferiority of others, because there is this transpersonal element of human consciousness that is severely violated by these projections. The lower the spiritual development, the more excluding it is. It is all too common for people to get stuck in those lower stages of spiritual development that say, "We have the truth and they don't." Conversely, the higher the spiritual development, the more inclusive it is, not only of fellow human beings but of all other living organisms.

If someone were to ask me what the Self is like, to show them a good representation of the Self, the best response I could give would be to say, "The Self is like a rabbi who lived in Jerusalem 2,000 years ago."

When we attempt to concretize the message of Jesus of Nazareth, or the message of the community that evolved around him, we lose something very important about his teachings and what he represented. It is said that Jesus spoke in parables and never wrote down his teachings because he wanted them to remain alive and fluid, transmitted from one person to another, and from one generation to another, through breath as a carrier of spirit.

We lose even more when we attempt to dismiss the myth of Christ as the story of some megalomaniac who pulled off the world's greatest hoax, claiming a virgin birth and resurrection that are both humanly impossible.

As Jung said, "We must learn to discern the difference between physical fact and spiritual truth."[1] The virgin birth and postgrave resurrection of Christ may not be true on the outside, but they are enduring spiritual truths with inner validity and resonance, speaking to us about incarnation of the divine in every human being, and about the resurrectional gift of grace, which makes it possible to begin again even in the midst of the greatest loss imaginable.

It doesn't take much research to discover that most of the charismatic manna personalities who have constellated projections of the Self throughout the millennia came into the world through extraordinary births, according to their myths. There is another mythological template in which the hero is sacrificed so that his people might survive and prosper. There is in all of these manna figures something of the prophetic Hermeneutic principle, a reference to the Greek messenger Hermes, who translated the will of the gods in a way so that mortals could understand. There is also a messianic element, which provides us not with a fulfillment, but instead with a promise of an ending that is yet to come.

These characteristics tend to put Jesus into a category of cultural heroes, which makes the fundamentalists very nervous, because they don't want Jesus placed into any category, except that of unique, exclusive, and exhaustive Truth. For Jesus to share the spotlight with other heroes makes literalists very anxious, but for me it is very liberating. Seeing the archetypal underpinnings of the Christian myth doesn't make it any less true or valuable. It's exactly the opposite. For me, identifying Christ's myth as a universal archetype is affirming, liberating, and empowering, for I can see that his myth has underpinnings that go far deeper than a small desert tribe in the first century. It is the song of the universe incarnated, speaking to the universal human psyche in a way that is true for every time and place.

We no longer have to scurry around trying to prove that biblical events really happened, like the poor guy who has spent millions searching for the remains of Noah's ark on Mt. Ararat. Nor do we need to concern ourselves with disproving the mythological stories, such as those who have suggested that ancient meteorological conditions led to wind parting the waters of the Red Sea or created the ice floe that Jesus floated upon, when it looked for all the world as if he were walking on water. All we need to ask ourselves is, "Does this myth resonate with our experience of what it means to be human?" "Does the myth offer us something to which we aspire?"

## THE GIFTS OF PARADOX

Jung stressed that human consciousness by its nature does not want to bear the inherent tension of a paradox, defined as a proposition that appears to be self-contradictory and inconsistent, such as the assertion that two things may be opposites but they may also both be true. Holding a paradox consciously, which is to say without making a judgment or taking sides, appears just too difficult and laborious for the ego to accept, at least willingly.

It is almost against our nature to hold two opposites consciously, because the ego, as a differentiating organ, wants to discern differences and make connections, an impulse that serves us for physical survival but not for spiritual growth. The ego's natural viewpoint is "either/or," while the paradox whispers "either and or." It offers the growth that is to be found in contemplating truths such as when we give, we shall receive; when we empty ourselves, we shall be filled; and when we lose ourselves, we shall be found.

If we are to live in the kingdom of God, we must learn to carry paradoxes consciously, for what could be a greater paradox than to be fully God and fully human at the same time, as Christ was, and as we all are?

Of all the Christian doctrines, the idea of Jesus Christ being fully human and fully God is most important to us in terms of its psychological profundity. Whether you buy into that is not necessary, but what is necessary is to understand the wisdom of positing such a paradox. Holding this paradox consciously is a model for the very nature of the Self; it is almost emblematic of what it means to be human. Are we divine or are we human? The answer to that is yes. To hold the paradox consciously is to find the growth and the wisdom we are searching for.

That's what I love so much about the Christmas story—the very idea that we would have a sacred story that says God's spiritual nature can enter into human beings. It seems to me that we take a little more responsibility for our own existence when we realize that we are carrying the essence of God, the Creator, the Source of the mystery within this finite quantum of energy we call the human organism.

It also makes people very nervous when we talk about the divine nature of humans, but this is very much what Jesus taught. One reason the church has long discouraged this kind of consciousness is that it can cause people to become inflated, to feel like not only do we carry the numinous energy of the Creator within ourselves, but that we may actually be able to act on that by dominating others, in essence playing God. There's an old saying that goes, "We don't worship God because God needs to be worshipped, we worship God so we don't worship ourselves." I think there is some truth to that, but the church has erred too far on the opposite extreme, encouraging us to feel deflated and devaluated about the prospect of being merely, miserably human.

Another reason for promoting the Augustinian doctrine of original sin and the Calvinistic viewpoint of our depraved humanity is that this theology has helped the institutional church maintain its role as a negative, shaming parent and hence its ability to control an infantilized flock. The church has feared that if people realized they had a divine nature within themselves, they wouldn't bother coming to church. I don't think that fear has foundation, because if the church was truly the church, it wouldn't see its role as keeping people dependent, but would instead see itself as an empowering resource for independence. When people attend church out of dependence or fear, the church tends to stay mired in anachronistic and archaic behavior. But when people attend church out of independence, important things happen both individually and collectively.

One of the messages we get from the transformed consciousness of the kingdom within is that being human is not a bad thing to be. It's difficult, to be sure, and filled of choices and mistakes, for it is impossible to be perfect, despite the exhortation in Matthew that, "You must be perfect, just as your father in heaven is perfect." Once again the true meaning of a profound biblical passage has been lost in translation. The trouble here is with the word *perfect*, which reflects the modern idea of one-sided pureness, a description of a person with nary a sinful thought or emotion.

In the original Greek verse, however, instead of *perfect*, the word *teleos* was used. Teleos literally means "brought to completion," and from this word we get *teleology*, which is the study of the completion of things. Another way of saying that something is brought to completion is that is has been made whole. This led Sanford to conclude that the original translation of this verse was, "You must therefore be whole, just as your father in heaven is whole."

This gives us a much different meaning than *perfect*, and if we ponder the teleological aspect of this verse, we can see that Jesus is urging us to be brought—to bring ourselves—to wholeness or completion. This viewpoint also sheds light on the age-old problem of how God, the transcendent Creator of the universe, can be a personal living reality for each human being. The answer is that he or she is as personal to each of us as our own inner creative process.

Along with modeling for his community how to lead a balanced and integrated human life, Jesus also offered valuable teachings about the nature of God and the nature of being human. Another one of Campbell's four functions of myth is that it helps us to understand the nature of being human, and how can we possibly understand human nature without understanding the psyche? Realizing this, scholars such as Sanford have tried to unlock the psychological truth of the Christian myth as a map to the inner world.

There is fairly universal agreement among religious scholars that the parables of Jesus are the closest we can get to what he actually said. In many cases, we have the parables alongside the interpretation of what they meant, and interpretations are generally the weakest link.

Sanford and others have concluded that when Jesus talked about the kingdom of God, he was talking synonymously about the kingdom within, about something that was within the reach of human experience. To use a language system from another culture, the kingdom of God is the same as the Dao, as Karma, as the Buddhist practice of living mindfully. It is what Johnson called the "golden world." Our attempts to describe the kingdom within and its counterparts with mere words are hopelessly inadequate, because our words are only symbols pointing to mysteries of such magnitude and paradox that we are never able to fully grasp and define them.

We can only suffice to say that the kingdom within is a kind of consciousness or viewpoint, a kind of knowing that has much in common with Gnosticism, an early branch of Christianity that emphasized self-knowledge as a path to knowing God. It is very interesting that Gnosticism has recently reappeared in the collective consciousness after many centuries of being repressed by the church as heretical. Derived from the Greek word *gnosis*, which means knowing, Gnosticism embraced a philosophical worldview that framed events such as the virgin birth and resurrection as symbolic rather than literal, and the tradition celebrated both the male and female elements of the divine. It has been suggested that Gnosticism may have been influenced by Hindu and Buddhist mystics, but regardless of whether that cross-fertilization actually happened, it is indeed a very Eastern-oriented religious viewpoint. In the Gnostic text *Dialogue of the Savior*, for example, a saying attributed to Jesus is, "Light the lamp within you," which bears a beautiful synchronicity with the Buddha's urging to "be a lamp unto yourself."

The early orthodox Christian church went to great lengths to discredit and suppress Gnostic viewpoints and to destroy Gnostic texts, but the discovery of an urn full of Gnostic Gospels at Nag Hammadi in northern Egypt in 1945 has propelled the Gnostic worldview back into the spotlight, at least among religious scholars. The Gnostic Gospels are filled with verses that support the concept of the kingdom within, such as this jewel from the Gospel of Thomas, in which Jesus admonished those who viewed the kingdom of God in literal terms, believing it to be a specific place. "If those who lead you say to you, 'Look, the Kingdom is in the sky,' then the birds will arrive there before you," Jesus said. Likewise, he says, if they say the Kingdom of God is in the sea, then the fish will arrive before you. Rather, Jesus said,

The Kingdom is inside of you, and it is outside of you. When you come to know yourselves, then you will be known, and you will realize that you are the sons of the living Father. But if you will not know yourselves, then you dwell in poverty, and it is you who are that poverty.[2]

From another tradition, and from our own time, the Zen Buddhist teacher Thich Nhat Hanh offers us this insight into the kingdom, which his religion calls the pure land of the Buddha:

We don't have to wait until we die to go to the Kingdom of Heaven; in fact, we have to be very alive. The Kingdom of God isn't just an idea; it's a reality, available to us in the full moon, the blue sky, the majestic mountains and rivers, and the beautiful faces of our children. We need only to be present.[3]

And he concludes: "The Kingdom of God is always available to us. But are we available to the Kingdom?"

There is a lot of evidence to suggest that Jesus really did believe that one must listen and follow one's own inner voice, and that when he refers to "my Father," he is really talking about the voice of the Self.

Jung was fascinated by Gnostic ideas, and he called continued modern-day disparagement of Gnosticism an anachronism. He believed that Gnostic ideas expressed "the other side of the mind," the nonrational side. The religious scholar Elaine Pagels describes these as "the spontaneous, unconscious thoughts that any orthodoxy requires its adherents to suppress."

Jung loved that line from the Gospel of Thomas, where Jesus came across men who were plucking grain on the Sabbath and said, "If thou knowest what thou doest thou art blessed. If thou not knowest thou art cursed." The point being that if you act consciously, as your own authority, then the ethic of the Self is a more reliable guide to responsible and moral conduct than any external code.

I would tend to agree with Pagels that the suppression of Gnosticism and many other forms of Christianity was probably inevitable and perhaps even necessary if Christianity were to survive through an era in which its existence and legitimacy were under constant attack by Jews and pagans alike. The Nicene creed, adopted at the First Council of Nicaea in 325, established conformity for Christian doctrine, selecting which texts would be included in the Bible, setting up the system of apostolic succession as the church's claim to legitimacy and authority, and declaring any nonconforming expressions of faith as heretical.

The decisions made at the council, during a period when patriarchy was consolidating its grip on Western consciousness, paved the way for Christianity to grow as a catholic, or universal, faith, but a steep price was paid when the religion's feminine and mystical nature was suppressed. Even as Jung described Christianity as a powerful archetypal compensation and a great gift to human consciousness, he cautioned that the religion had become one-sided in favor of the masculine Logos, the logical or thinking way of being, with little or no value placed on the feminine Eros, the nonrational or feeling way of being, that love force of life.

Jung said that Christianity had also become unbalanced in the orthodox claim that God's revelation had ended in Christ. He sided with the Gnostics, who believed that revelation was a continuing process that would bring forth change and evolution, not only in traditions and institutions, but also in individuals. *Incarnation* means "God come in flesh," and in this way of thinking, there would be a continuing incarnation of God in each human being as that person became whole, and thus holy.

Jung saw Gnosticism as a way of restoring Christianity's lost vitality, as a bridge that could help many people cross over to a more living appreciation of the Christian tradition. The renewed interest in Gnostic ideas appears to be part of a great paradigm shift in human consciousness that he predicted for the twenty-first century. Jung called this new consciousness the *New Age*, although this term has been trivialized into a catchall phrase for anything that is new or outside the mainstream. This is not to say that these things are necessarily bad or not of value, but they aren't what Jung was talking about when he created the term *New Age*.

There are a thousand ways to describe the new kind of consciousness that Jung saw emerging, but at it most basic level, the New Age is a postmodern awareness that recognizes anew the value of the nonrational and the non-material, thus balancing many centuries of devaluing these aspects in favor of the rational and the material. This new consciousness places value on the symbolic life and the inner world, which includes the kingdom within. Included, too, is a rebirth of the feminine consciousness, or the feminine archetype, which is much more concerned with the mystical, nonrational, and nonmaterial than its male counterpart. We are thirsty for a more spiritual way of being that the feminine consciousness can offer, and that's why there is so much interest in drinking from this well.

So similar to the Gnostic or New Age viewpoint, the kingdom within is a way of being or perceiving oneself in the world. Not to be confused with education, intelligence, or thinking, it is a kind of consciousness that authenticates life and looks for meaning. It values mystery, curiosity, and spontaneity. Rather than being closed off with the aridity of certainty, this consciousness is open, fluid, and charismatic, with a deep appreciation for all that is subtle, novel, or ambiguous. It is a kind of awareness that takes delight in those precious moments of the human experience, when the transcendent integrates with the mundane in a way that is both imminent and immediate. We live in the kingdom of God within our own journey, our own psyche, and our own process of individuation, all the while simultaneously living in outer world. This state of consciousness does not take you away from the world, but rather empowers you to be more fully present in the world in a way that is healthier and more abundant.

Most of us can identify with the language of being "born again," and Church likens initiation into the kingdom of God as a kind of second birth, awakening from a deep and dreamless sleep to find oneself in a great cathedral:

> This second birth, at once miraculous and natural, is in some ways not unlike the first...Such awakenings may happen only once in a lifetime, or many times. But when they do, what you took for granted before is presented as a gift: difficult, yet precious and good.[4]

In the kingdom of God, we must learn be nonrational, for there is a whole other dimension of life that is just as valuable as the rational, or perhaps more so. There is a different kind of arithmetic, a different kind of physics that is beyond the grasp of our limited consciousness. Now we're beginning to think those things that aren't matter may be those things that matter most, that the nonmaterial may be as important as the material. There is a kind of nonrational, nonmaterial economy operating in the kingdom of God, so that the last shall be first, that those who work one hour get paid the same as those who work all day, and that the rain falls on the just and unjust, as Christ taught us.

The thing we hunger for most is some sense that this enterprise that we're in, this human vocation that comes with a birth we didn't request and a grave we can't escape, that it has meaning and purpose. We want to know that we have a reason for being here. The kingdom of God is the consciousness that says, "Yes, this human vocation is a valuable enterprise, and I'm making a contribution, which is to become my true Self as authentically as Christ became his true Self."

In the kingdom of God, we're beginning to realize that evolution is about consciousness, and that the greatest contribution we can make to the world is to become fully conscious. We're beginning to realize that being human is a worthy vocation in its own right, and that the value of our life is not about seeking money, power, or control, nor is it about simply surviving. That's not where the meaning is. The meaning is in the authenticity, in one becoming oneself.

## WHERE IS THE KINGDOM?

I carry the kingdom of God within me, and paradoxically I am simultaneously living within the kingdom of God. A closer look at the Bible can shed a little light on this paradox.

In the New Testament, Jesus talks about the kingdom of God in three different ways. Sometimes he talks about the kingdom of God as being in the midst of you. So if we were all standing around in a circle, the kingdom would be at the center. Other times, he tells us that the kingdom of God is among us, suggesting that it is transpersonal. To use the analogy of the circle again, the kingdom would be within each of us, while simultaneously it is also in the midst of us. Lastly, Jesus says that the kingdom of God is within me, and you. So back in the circle, the kingdom is within me, it is within the midst of us, and it is among us. Speaking from another tradition, Carl Rogers said that which is most personal is most universal, and that offers us a nice insight into the archetypal nature of the kingdom of God. It is within me, I am within it, and it is within us, all at the same time. We are in it, and it lives within us.

If we look back at how the original text of the Bible has been translated over the ages, we can see how the church's devaluation of the human being— itself an evolving attitude—has influenced the course of theology. Sanford argues that Luke 17 originally read, "The Kingdom of God is within you," but that "within" was later changed to "among." He argued:

> This choice of translation betrays the extraverted attitude of our time, which finds it hard to conceive that anything worthwhile could be within us. In the early church, however, this passage was invariably rendered as "within." Being closer to (Christ's) time, the church fathers were closer to his spirit and knew of the reality of the inner world.[5]

Although highly personal to the individual, the kingdom of God is open to all. It knows of no race, creed, gender, sexual orientation, or social status. Jesus Christ himself says that many will come from the east and west to take their places at the feast of the kingdom of God.

The fourth function of myth, to borrow again from Campbell's list, is that it helps us to understand human psychology. In this framework, we can see Christ is a symbol of the Self, and we can see the kingdom within as an archetypal awareness which informs us of another inner world or reality, one that is going on simultaneously with the consensus reality we experience as the outer world. Being conscious of this inner reality can help us live in the outer world in a healthier, more meaningful way. It is the world of the flesh and of the spirit, the material and the nonmaterial, and the rational and the nonrational. It is about time that we realized that all of these realities are part of the nature of being human.

From the viewpoint of depth psychology and, I would add, profound twenty-first-century theology, the message of the Christian myth is that we are to take authority for our own lives, in the way Jesus took authority for his own life, even when it costs us our life. I would rather think about that symbolically rather than literally, but it does seem like anybody who tries to take authority for their own life, particularly a manna personality on which the is Self has been projected, is going to get killed, or at least suffer grievously.

Taking responsibility for our own lives is far different from saviorhood, the expectation that there is somebody out there who will get me out of this anxiety-filled human existence, if I am willing to abdicate my autonomy and decision-making authority. I think that's an OK solution for those who want such an easy answer to all of the fears and anxieties that are inherent to being human, but the only problem is you miss your life.

## HOW DO YOU ENTER THE KINGDOM?

Many know what Jesus said in Matthew 19, "It is easier for a camel to go through the eye of a needle than for a rich man to enter the Kingdom of Heaven." We cannot buy or muscle our way into the kingdom, so how do we get there? Self-confrontation is a necessity, as Jesus made clear in his parable of the prodigal son. I mentioned earlier that our sacred stories are the jewels that Eve smuggled out of Eden, that they are kaleidoscopic jewels that shimmer with new revelations and insights each time you examine them.

The prodigal son is a shining example of this. One of its facets is the message that each of us has a pharisaic older brother side who presents an opposite viewpoint to our younger wayward son side, and in this dynamic, we can see how self-confrontation helps us to know our own nature and to evolve that nature. (The Pharisees are frequently depicted in the New Testament as legalistic, self-righteous rule-followers more concerned with the letter of the law rather than its spirit. Where Jesus emphasized God's love and sought out sinners, the Pharisees were obsessed with man-made laws and scorned sinners. There has been some debate about whether this depiction of the Pharisees is anti-Semitic, but for our purposes, it applies to the hypocritical and arrogant part of our own personality, and not any external group or being.)

Although the kingdom of heaven is not mentioned in this parable, it is clearly a parable of the kingdom, as well as a cornerstone of Jesus's attitude. The paradox of the parable is that each of the two brothers represents two sides of one whole person. We are simultaneously the prodigal who leaves and goes into the outer world to have all of the subsequent experiences, and we are also the resentful older brother who stays home.

We are the brother who conforms and adapts to the rules and guidelines, identifying with our tribe and family of origin rather than our own individual autonomy. At the same time, we are the autonomous one who leaves all of that to seek our inheritance and finally recognizes the wisdom of coming back to integrate with the part of ourself we left behind.

The parable of the prodigal son is one of many sacred stories that tell us about somebody who is forced to leave his tribe or family. This mythological formula is a re-presentation of the psychological evolution that is going on within each of us.

In analyzing these stories, it is helpful to consider that the relationship of the ego to the unconscious is the same as the relationship of the fetus to the womb, as Adam and Eve to the garden of Eden, and as Abraham to Moses. There's always a kind of birthing, which is also to say a kind of leaving, going on in these relationships, which parallel the evolution of human consciousness. The fetus leaves the womb, later to become a child who leaves the mother, who becomes a young adult who leaves the peer group, and so on. We have Adam and Eve leaving the Garden of Eden, and we have Jesus sauntering along the Sea of Galilee, telling the crowds that "you must leave your family and come follow me."

This same process also plays out constantly in our own consciousnesses, where some part of the ego is always leaving the unconscious as it slowly and incrementally evolves and develops. Simultaneously, we are giving birth at the same time we are dealing death. Paradoxically, we are finishing and leaving, at the same time that we are also beginning and returning. This is heart of the psychological truth that the myths are trying to tell us. They inform us that it is unwise and unhealthy to stay in one place, as if that were even possible to begin with. They speak to us about being evicted from places of comfort, and we resist these forced departures with all our might, even though growth and transformation can only begin when we leave the known and the familiar.

The ego wants to romanticize, idealize, and sentimentalize the process of individuation, or the journey to the kingdom within, but the hard fact remains that it is not so much a journey as a calling. It is not an elite or special calling, but rather it is only a particular calling. It does seem to have special appeal, however, to those who have somehow received more than their fair share of wounding in life. My own experience is that most periods of enlightenment begin with some kind of crisis, accident, or loss, and people who have been injured in some way are the ones who are most interested in individuation, consciousness, living mindfully, or the kingdom within.

We can generalize and say to be human is to be injured. But some of us have found particularly painful losses early in life, or we experience a series of events that continue to wound us and compel us to seek consciousness, whether they be job loss, divorce, accidents, illness, or addiction. As I'm fond of saying, grace enters the soul through our wounds, so fortunate are the wounded if they are able to view their injuries as openings to a new level of consciousness.

A person who has not recognized her need or despair is not ready for the kingdom of God, nor are those who feel that they are self-sufficient or who remain caught in their one-sided egocentricity. This is why Jesus associated with out-groups such as sinners and tax collectors (then as now an unpopular bunch) and was generally unable to have a relationship with the Pharisees, who as a rule were upheld by their egocentricity, privileged position in society, and conviction of their own righteousness. What the ego wants is to survive and prosper, not to suffer. It is much more likely to want entertainment, security, and structure than to follow the wisdom of Jesus' hard sayings or to pay the cost of discipleship. Whether it is a Pharisee or a modern-day conservative, it is very rare for anybody to want to change a system that has rewarded them with privilege, status, and wealth. The ones who want to change the system, or find another system altogether, are those of us who have experienced some systemic injury.

In *How the Irish Saved Civilization*, the historian Thomas Cahill says that Jesus was attracted to "oddball, off-center" personalities: "In the Gospel story, the passionate, the outsized, the out-of-control have a better shot at seizing heaven that the contained, the calculating, and those of whom this world approves."[6]

Johnson, too, has noted that anyone who undergoes a growth in consciousness is immediately assailed by the culture, especially its masculine elements, which are particularly hostile to any change in consciousness or consensus. "It has been said that Jesus had no trouble with the women near him but came to grief with the prevailing masculine law and order of his time," he writes.[7]

If we consider that the original Greek work for *character* meant "distinctive mark," we can see that the Self and character are synonyms for a person who has reached, or is reaching toward, his or her individuation. So that when somebody is living out their distinctive mark, they are usually referred to as a character, whether they are as noticeably different as Forrest Gump or simply one of those people who are, with oh-so-subtle condescension, called artsy or unique. People who truly become themselves tend to be marginalized or derided, because they have left the tribe and its system of adaptation and conformity. Thus the price of discipleship in the kingdom of God is high. If you make becoming conscious and following your own way a priority, the cost is often loneliness and being misunderstood.

I have empathy for the characters of the world because, while many people would look at me and consider me to be successful by most measures, I too have experienced subtle forms of marginalization. I have been told over and over again by sincere, well-meaning people, "Pittman, with the way you speak and articulate things, you would have made a great lawyer." Or, "You would have made a great corporate executive." What are these people really saying to me? They are saying that what I do—counseling and speaking about the world of symbols and the inner life—is a waste of time or, at best, an indulgence. The implication is that what I do is not of value. It's irrational and immaterial, and certainly not businesslike. I may be a real character, but I wouldn't have it any other way.

The adverse relationship between privilege, wealth, and the kingdom of God is expressed in the parable of the wedding feast, in which the king held a lavish banquet in honor of his son's upcoming marriage. First, he invited the most respected members of the community, but they were all too busy and engrossed in their own affairs to accept the king's invitation. The monarch thus became angry and said those who had been invited had proved to be unworthy, and he ordered his servants to go to the crossroads and invite everybody else they could find. The Gospel of Luke recounts how the feast hall was thus filled with the poor, crippled, blind, and lame, for the king wanted to make sure his house was full for this special occasion.

To many people, the punishment of excluding the good townspeople seems harsh and cruel, but we must remember there is no room for sentimentality in the kingdom of God. Christianity is a deeply feeling religion that engages our emotions as well as our intellect, but one thing it is not is a sentimental religion. This sentimentalizing of the feeling aspect of Christianity has been one of the disasters that have overtaken the Christian spirit. Exemplified by the overly sweet and cloying Norman Rockwell view of Christmas and Easter, the one-sided sentimental viewpoint offers no possibility of new life that can be gained only through the pain of birth and the cost of death.

Part of the reason I personally have no love for sentimentally is that its opposite is brutality, and like any pair of opposites at either extreme of a continuum, they exist very close to one another and can quickly flip to become each other. Once you push the sentimental religion of the idealized sweet baby Jesus far enough, it can become as brutal as hell. You have people who want you to know this sweet, gentle, peaceful Jesus so desperately, they will kill you if you don't receive him. The oversentimentalizing of Christianity denies the inconvenient truth that there is no grace without disgrace, no Easter without Good Friday. The sentimentalists have gotten stuck in an infantile dependency that makes an idol of out Jesus, rather than listening to what the man said through his parabolic teachings.

In the kingdom of God, we are given the hard spiritual facts, with no room or tolerance for sentiment. If we jump off a cliff, we will surely break a leg. This is a physical fact, and we have no reason to expect God to interfere with our fate if we flout the physical facts of his creation, namely, gravity and the fragility of our human flesh and bones. There are also spiritual facts, which are as real and objective as physical facts. One of the most important is that if we insist on remaining unconscious, despising and devaluing the inner world, then we can expect to be treated ruthlessly by the unconscious, because in our refusal to become conscious, we flout the law of the kingdom of God, which insists that we seek consciousness as our life task.

CHAPTER 8

# THE (LIGHTER) BURDEN
# OF CONSCIOUSNESS

Jesus said, "Do not suppose I am come to bring peace to the earth, but a sword."

The sword here is a symbol of psychological discernment, rather than an instrument of physical impaling. Jesus wanted us to differentiate from the group identification, and he wanted us to plunge ourselves into the inner fire. In the Gospel of Thomas, Jesus says, "Whoever is near to me is near to the fire, whoever is far from me is far from the Kingdom." Following our thesis that Jesus is a symbol of the Self, this passage could be translated as, "Whoever is near to the Self is near to the fire, whoever is far from the Self is far from the Kingdom."

The group protects, indeed prevents, us from coming into contact with the fiery nature of Selfhood, a nature that is paradoxically both destructive and transformative. Only when one has been consumed by fire can one be reborn like the mythical phoenix, or resurrected like Jesus of Nazareth.

Jesus also promised to set us against our parents, which may not make sense in the outer world, but is a wise and necessary step in the inner world. The process of becoming an individual necessarily involves a separation from family identification. To become our true selves, we must become free from any unconscious identification with our parents, spouse, or siblings, as well as our larger tribe or community. Identifying with individuals or groups keeps us from becoming ourself.

According to some very wise men, including Jesus Christ, Carl Jung, and John Sanford, we are called to live our lives from the inside out, not from the outside in, even if that means struggling with an institutionalized religion that has placed all of God on the outside. In other words, the authority must come from within, from the inner divine being—God, or the Self—who reigns over the kingdom within, and not from a God image we have projected externally and attached to a religious structure.

The truth of who we are comes from inside each of us, and only by getting in contact with our inner world can we discover our true vocation. I use vocation to mean one's true calling in life, which is not to be confused (or trivialized) by associating it with our career. Like the lawyer in the earlier chapter who felt called to teach and coach, we all have an inner voice that reveals to us our true calling, if only we are willing and able to listen. And as was evident in this man's story, the thought of heeding the voice of the Self is often accompanied by one or more paralyzing complexes, which usually have to do with the great fear of not conforming and adapting to please our families and the larger culture.

Jesus proved to be a very wise analytical psychologist for counseling us about the need to separate from our families of origin and all the other systems that can keep us from claiming our own authority and autonomy. Jesus wasn't urging us to literally all be neurotic Lone Rangers, but rather he was talking about the idea that if you are going to follow your calling, if you are going to be a disciple of the kingdom of God, then you must stop trying to conform and adapt and instead find your own path. This sounds idealistic and romantic, but in fact, it is very difficult. At the same time, it is imperative.

In order to bring forth our inner content, separation is crucial, but most often we don't know how to make a clean cut with the sword, as Jesus was able to do. Usually, the only way we know how to separate is to go about it unconsciously, creating a crisis that will get us out of a situation, such as having an affair to escape a stifling marriage. Tragically, people also (and almost always unconsciously) use violence to get out of places where they feel trapped, such as turning a literal rather than a symbolic sword against their own families. Most often, however, we unconsciously turn against that most convenient and familiar victim, our own self. The rampant malaise of depression is nothing but anger turned inward, and often we also make ourselves physically sick from the inner violence we do to ourselves. At the extreme end, we end our own lives if we can come up with no other way to get out of our suffering.

Great crowds heard Jesus say, "If any man comes to me without hating his mother, father, wife, children, brother, sisters, and his own life too, he cannot be my disciple."

It may seem strange that Jesus points to the family as an enemy, but sometimes there is so much love and loyalty to one's own family or tribe that they can become enemies to the kingdom of God, obstacles to individuation. We have no difficulty in denying what we dislike for the kingdom, but to deny that which is closest to us, that which has earned our most extreme loyalty, is very difficult. This is not to suggest that we literally leave our families or never form family bonds as adults, but it is to raise the idea that the dark side of a close family is that it is difficult or impossible to separate from.

Often, when a strong identification with our family is thwarting our individuation, this motif of hating our families appears in our dreams. The dream in which we reject mother or father, or fight with those we feel close to, represents the need to break with an unconscious identification with a family figure. Fighting, quarreling, and struggling with those we feel close to expresses the unconscious urge to differentiate ourselves psychologically, so that we may become free as individuals.

I describe this dream with the permission of the dreamer, my son Jarrett, who came downstairs one morning when he was about 14, wearing a strange expression on his face, looking almost guilty or ashamed. I asked him what the matter was, and he recounted a disturbing dream in which he had killed his mother with a baseball bat. When he finished, I said, "What a wonderful, significant dream. It is telling you exactly what you need to do." Killing your mother—not a good idea on the outside. But what a healthy, appropriate thing to do on the inside, especially when you have reached the age, as my son had at the time, when it is appropriate to begin transferring the authority from the parental figure to the peer group, which is an interim developmental step before you can ultimately become your own authority.

About the price of discipleship in the kingdom of heaven, Sanford wrote, "It makes demands on us and allows us to place no other value in life higher than the calling to consciousness." That statement may sound dramatic or romantic, but it is not. To decide that there is no value higher than consciousness is a very costly decision to make, so costly that many are called and few choose. I'm very empathic with this viewpoint, but for me, accepting the call to discipleship in the kingdom within is not an either/or proposition, although I agree that strong language is necessary when describing the priority we must assign to becoming conscious, for there is so much competition for our attention, so many distractions, so many excuses to remain unconscious. Like any paradox, choosing the call to consciousness presents a case where two things can be true at once, and I'm going to disagree with Sanford a little here.

Individuation may be the single most important archetypal urge we possess, and it may ultimately be the urge that must prevail, but it is not the only one. Almost equally strong is the archetypal urge we have to make family, to belong to a clan where we have a place and feel loved, honored, and valued. A very subjective, even radical, Jungian viewpoint would be that I am my own self-contained family, carrying my parents, children, and significant other all within my inner world. On a certain level, this is true, but we cannot deny the archetypal drive to be in family with others. This makes it difficult to place the call to individuate above all else, for it often means leaving our home, family, job, and the security of the known.

I have great empathy for all those parts of myself that have for so long resisted individuation. It's not about us and them. It's about us. We are they. Each of us has made compromises on one side or another for family, children, or someone else who's dependent on us. We've sacrificed some of our own true nature, our own calling, to belong. I accept and honor that. We can't judge anyone—least not ourselves—for making choices when there are two nearly equally strong archetypal urges.

In a perfect world, we would be able to individuate within our family, in a family system that would be supportive and provide mutual respect for the autonomy of every member. This rarely happens, however, because we only have other humans to be in family with, and we all know how imperfect and territorial humans can be. I reiterate that there really aren't any systems I know of that model or promote autonomy, consciousness, and individuation, and this includes the family system. Most of the systems we have are set up to promote adaptation and conformity, and they work very effectively. The irony is that the more one individuates, the more one becomes a part of the collective, and if we had a truly healthy collective, it's job would be to empower the individual.

The ideal would be to journey at home, and to be at home on the journey. The only problem is that I don't live in an ideal world. I live in a world of ambiguity and ambivalence, where I am never quite able to see what will always be the healthy thing, the ideal thing, the best thing, the right thing to do. I get two truths, and I want them both, or I get two untruths, and I don't want either. I don't have the kind of clarity I daydream about having, and I pray for that sword of decisiveness, discernment, and clarity, so that I may know the right thing to do in every circumstance. I don't always get it, and I am not immune to regressing occasionally and wanting somebody to give me the answers.

When we talk about the journey—a metaphor for individuation—we often get overly romantic and sentimental. The ego loves this romantic idealism. It yearns to be like Frodo, to grab the ring and set off on the journey, but most of us are too human to live the idealized life because in the end we can only live the human life, with all the limited knowledge and capabilities that implies.

A few years ago, I gave a lecture I called "The Non-Sentimental Journey," where I talked about how, little by little, each of our life support systems is taken away from us, beginning around midlife. Whether we set out to consciously make individuation a priority, invariably life will take care of a lot of this by attrition, so that eventually we are left alone with the task we tried so hard to avoid, and it stares us in the face. As we leave home, as our children leave home, as our marriages and careers hit the rocks and fall apart, our task for the second half of life gradually presents itself clearly to us, like an iceberg emerging from the fog. It begins to tug—if not tear—at our consciousness.

Our work for the second half of life is to reconnect the ego to the Self, and to place the ego in proper relationship to the Self, which invariably means a painful demotion for this inflated, anxious organ of consciousness. All of our ego attachments—our job titles, degrees, trophy homes, second homes, trophy spouses, mistresses, and other possessions—are the very stuff of codependency. They are signs that we cannot generate life for ourselves, so we try to prop up our sense of self by desperately clinging to things that exist outside of us.

The only problem is that these things do not last. Just like with chewing gum, the initial sweetness goes away pretty quickly, and pretty soon we find ourselves just routinely chewing a flavorless glob, at the same time wondering why we can't seem to just spit it out and find something that would be truly fulfilling. At midlife, life puts us in a harsh, unforgiving kind of intensive care unit, where all of our life-support systems—job, spouse, children, and illusions—are systematically unplugged, one at a time. The life-and-death question is, "Will the patient be able to survive and prosper on his own?"

I talk a lot about family in this metaphor, which is not to devalue family at all, because it's very important for us to be in family and to value family. It's part of our archetypal impulse for survival. But it's quite another thing to be codependent on family. If I am dependent on my mother and father to generate life for me, they are dead or will die. If I am dependent on my children, they have left home. If I am dependent on my job, that foundation is about as sturdy as quicksand, especially in today's economy.

Achieving independence means that I can generate life from inside of myself, not from outside sources such as my parents, job, bank account, spouse, or children. All of these things will pass away, leave home, wear out, or at least radically change.

For many people, a gnawing dissatisfaction with their career is what first signals the call to individuation, since in our extraverted, work-obsessed culture, our American religion promises us that our job will generate life for us. This is a false promise, for it is only our true vocation or calling that will generate life and creativity. I have often said that the first half of life is biography, where we allow our story to be written for us by others, in our understandable need to adapt and conform in order to survive. The second half of life must be autobiography, authored by the Self.

The rugged individualism of the American psyche also encourages us, especially if we are men, to set off on our journey alone. It is possible, but not probable, that we can do it by ourselves. When I talk about becoming your own independent authority, I don't mean that we need to become some solitary cowboy-type figure who thinks he can go it alone, with no help or support. We really need to be open to receiving guides and teachers, in our personal relationships and also in the myths. The paradox is that I alone must become myself, but I cannot become myself alone. Though we are ultimately responsible for becoming our own authorities, we need support and companions along the way.

Sanford writes about the heaviness of unconsciousness and the freedom we feel when we begin to engage the inner world and let in the light of consciousness:

> The unconscious is like a great weight when it affects us in a way we do not understand. One who has no relationship to his unconscious world...experiences it negatively as a dark burden. This heaviness of the unrealized inner world is suggested in dreams by the familiar motif of trying to run but finding it impossible, not being able to move, as affected by extreme inertia.
>
> On the other hand, when the inner world is consciously experienced, it can give to consciousness a first experience of freedom. To know the inner realm is to be freed from its heaviness and to experience its creativity. In this creativity lies our freedom. What once burdened us now gives us strength. We may now in our dreams make even a steep ascent with agility.[1]

Unconsciousness is a burden we are born with, and the process of becoming conscious is a burden we choose. The latter is a gift we give ourselves, for of the two burdens, consciousness is ultimately the lighter load, despite the arduousness of the task. To remain unconscious is a much greater burden, but many remain stuck in this darkness because the idea of becoming conscious is very threatening to those who are not willing to do the work or for some reason do not have the resources to do the work.

Becoming conscious just plain hurts, and anybody who courts pain is a masochist. But consciousness is not something we court; it is something we are called to. The one seemingly appropriate justification for the suffering that comes with the struggle for consciousness is that, evidently, this is the way the soul is built. For reasons I admit to not fully understanding, there seems to be no other way to get to consciousness except to suffer. It appears to be incumbent to the human condition. We're talking here about spiritual suffering, not the kind of physical suffering that should by all means be palliated with the appropriate medicine. We're talking about the soul suffering that comes from seeking the meaning in life, rather than being satisfied with all of life's distractions.

Let's remind ourselves that suffering comes from the Latin *ferrer*, which means "to carry from below." When we suffer something, we are literally standing under it, we are carrying it until we can understand it. That's where we get the word *understanding*. You stand under it until you can comprehend it.

Suffering is about understanding the meaning. It's very hard in the midst of something to understand the meaning of it, like when we're in the belly of the whale. There's too much pain, confusion, and ambivalence going on. The intensity is too great. It's often only in retrospect that we are able to understand something, and sometimes it's years later. And we always want to leave open the possibility there was no meaning, for there are meaningless events. Not many, but they do exist. Sometimes, after we've looked at something from every side and every direction, we can only say, "I'll be damned, I think it was meaningless." For most things, though, we can get close to the meaning, and it is surely worth the exercise. It's also nice to have companions along the way, to help us hold our arms up like Moses when we're trying to suffer things and carry them.

When Jesus talked about taking on the Pharisees, and he was talking about confronting the inner Pharisee within each of us. We all wear this mask of hypocrisy from time to time, which is the persona put on in order to adapt, survive, and ensure that people have the image of us that we want them to have. We occasionally wear this ego identification consciously, such as on occasions where we'd rather not spend the energy to argue or disagree, but most of the time we are unconscious.

We must give ourselves permission to take off our masks, and if we are to occasionally don a persona for whatever reason, this false self must take a backseat to the true Self. Our attitude toward ourselves must be one of unconditional love and self-acceptance, whatever our self-perceived faults might be.

That may sound like the kind of pop psychology you can find among the magazines at the supermarket checkout aisle, and it might seem like a self-help project that's easy, even fun, to take on. But let me tell you, in all my years of experience as a people helper, I have found that one of the most difficult things for people to do is to get rid of the radical double-standard they use against themselves. People will readily forgive, overlook, and understand things about other people, even huge and glaring faults, but they beat themselves up over their own slightest imperfection, even if that so-called imperfection exists only in their own mind and nobody else's. That is the voice of the negative father complex, the patriarchal viewpoint that we must be civilized until even the tiniest flaws have been wiped out of existence.

To practice self-acceptance, we must accept the inner enemy we have labeled as unacceptable. This advice usually comes as a shock to people who have been trained to reject themselves, especially in a culture such as ours that has made a fetish out of self-rejection. Centuries of the American religion, and centuries of St. Augustine and Calvin before that, have indoctrinated us with a self-image that we are depraved sinners, that evil springs from us, and that a large part of our personality is to be regarded as belonging to the devil. This attitude is everywhere and is one of the great maladies of our culture. For many, the Christian life is identical with a life in which one places no value whatsoever upon oneself. A true believer is supposed to efface oneself completely, placing value only on others and on God, hence the old saying, "God is first, others are second, and I am third."

Those striving for the kingdom of God are called to embrace self-acceptance, even for those parts of our personality that seem to be the lowest, most inferior, and devilish. It is no wonder the older brother didn't like the father's idea that he must welcome his younger brother, the prodigal son, back home. How can we accept a part of ourself that we have labeled shameful, worthless, and weak, when we would much rather not acknowledge it as our own?

The ethic of the kingdom of God is more paradoxical than we have ever dared let ourselves suppose. This ethic is not righteousness but love, not following the rules but accepting ourselves. These are the keys to the kingdom of God.

When Jesus was asked to name the greatest of the commandments, he cited the first, "You must love God with all your heart." The second commandment, "You must love thy neighbor," closely resembles it.

Our ability to love others seems to exist in direct proportion to our ability to love ourselves. The very idea that we could get to the place where we would see that loving ourselves would be the greatest thing we could do for everyone—that is a most exhilarating possibility! It is certainly the best thing you can do for Jesus, for with self-love comes self-acceptance and the freedom to be your authentic Self. It would be amazing how much our marriages and other relationships would improve, not to mention our careers and the world at large. To tweak an old saying, perhaps charity really does begin at home—in the inner world.

So the kingdom of God demands that we love ourselves. Not with the kind of autoerotic narcissism that our culture fosters, and which promotes the idea that I'm better, I'm special, I'm entitled. That kind of attitude is not love for Self or anyone else, but a transparent overcompensation for an inferiority complex. It's easy to love those parts of ourselves that we are proud of, but to truly love our whole Self means accepting and owning our inner enemy, our flawed humanity, and the instinctuality we have been told is so evil.

Jung felt strongly that, from a psychological viewpoint, we should begin to look at good and evil as paired opposites, and to see that the dynamic tension between these opposites has an observable function, which may paradoxically be to contribute to God's creation, or the evolution of our own consciousness.

In the vocabulary of Heraclitus, the pre-Socratic Greek philosopher, there is a dynamic of *enantiodromia* at work in the world, meaning that each force is constantly seeking its opposite, and that there is a tension in these forces as they run counter to each other, such as the tension between good and evil.

This dynamic often places us in a pivotal position, where we teeter on the brink of transcending to a new level or descending to a lower level of our development. The decision is ours to make.

Whatever we mean when we say God, this Creator is beyond good and evil, in Jung's viewpoint. God has let loose these the forces of good and evil in the universe, and the tension between them helps human beings to develop a kind of consciousness that would not be possible otherwise. It is difficult for many of us to accept that the Creator is the origin of both good and evil, because we want to see God as a pure, unbalanced force that is nothing but goodness. But if we reorient our vision and take away the judgment, we can say that the source of good and evil, like the source of everything, is the Creator, or Creatrix. If that is just too difficult, we can suffice to say that the source is a mystery.

The very idea of evil is reformulated in the kingdom of God, and Jesus took evil very seriously as a force. For him, evil existed in its own right as an independent, autonomous agency opposed to God. He himself confronted evil as this disembodied force during his temptations in the wilderness. The idea that man did not create evil, but that it came into and remains in existence on its own is a significant idea for the Christian tradition—and a radical departure from our ingrained way of thinking.

Man's choices are crucial in determining the final balance of good and evil, but these decisions in themselves do not create evil. Psychologically, our consciousness grows primarily in opposition to evil. We become conscious out of necessity, in order to overcome evil. So, in some paradoxical way, evil may serve some deep ultimate purpose of God. Good and evil are two polarities necessary if there's to be any spiritual meaning to creation.

Similarly, we need to reexamine the way we think about sin, which has also led us to an unnecessarily dark view of human nature. We derive the word *sin* from the Greek word *armatia*, which means to be "off the mark." So sin originally meant to be off the mark, or not true to your character, which also means "a distinctive mark." Jung said that the greatest sin is to remain unconscious, which means not coming to know your distinctive mark, not making decisions that are death-dealing to the ego, and not taking responsibility for the laborious, painful vocation of becoming conscious.

The Gnostics had much to say about the temptation to remain unconscious, as well as its consequences. Various Gnostic Gospels compare the state of unconsciousness to being ignorant, rootless, living in fog and oblivion. They likened the resistance to *gnosis*, "self-knowledge," to the desire to be asleep or drunk. The *Gospel of Truth* describes such an existence as a "nightmare" (remember Chekhov?) filled with "terror and confusion and instability and doubt and division."

"Self-ignorance is also a form of self-destruction," Pagels writes, setting up this excerpt from the *Dialogue of the Savior*, a Gnostic text: "If one does not [understand] how the fire came to be, he will burn in it, because he does not know his root...Whoever does not understand how he came will not understand how he will go."[2] Pagels describes a principal shared by the Gnostics and modern psychotherapy: "Both agree, against orthodox Christianity—that the psyche bears *within itself* [emphasis hers] the potential for liberation or destruction. Few psychiatrists would disagree with the saying attributed to Jesus in the Gospel of Thomas, 'If you bring forth what is within you, what you bring forth will save you. If you do not bring forth what is within you, what you do not bring forth will destroy you.'"[3]

Jung was very interested in positing evil as an undifferentiated force in the world, because this viewpoint helps us transcend the traditional idea that most of us were raised with, which is that sin came into the world out of human free will and our choice to disobey God. Sanford said that if all human beings disappeared in a moment, evil would still exist. It's an undifferentiated force, not just in humans, but in the world, working itself into human beings through the human experience.

The reason Jung, Sanford, and I are so concerned about revising the idea that evil comes into the world through humans is that this viewpoint sets up a self-consciousness that tells us something is fundamentally wrong with us. With this idea instilled into us beginning at a very early age, we actually begin to believe that we are deeply flawed, even depraved as Calvin would have us believe, and that redemption is only possible through a God who has sacrificed his only son. Psychologically, we would like to start over and say, "As human beings, we have a nature that can be dualistic unless we become conscious and integrate these paired opposites of good and evil." That would be a more realistic viewpoint of what it means to be human.

Augustine's doctrine of original sin was essentially a retelling of the creation story in Genesis I, where humankind was given the choice between maintaining our innocence and having the knowledge of good and evil. As one might guess, the wily feminine chose to want to know what God knows, and ever since, mankind has been symbolically denied the innocence represented by the Garden of Eden.

A Jungian analysis of this myth would view the serpent as representing instinctuality. It is our instinct to want to know what God knows. It is our instinctual programming, archetypally, that we want to become conscious. The warning in the myth of the Garden of Eden is that if we become conscious, it's costly. Pagels quotes the Gospel of Thomas to describe the "inner turmoil" (and ultimately the liberation) that accompanies self-discovery:

> Jesus said, "Let him who seeks continue seeking until he finds. When he finds, he will become troubled. When he becomes troubled, he will be astonished, and he will rule over all things."[4]

The myth tells us there are two things that God said would become natural consequences of becoming conscious. One, it is painful and laborious to try and reconcile the opposites that you didn't know existed moments before you chose to eat the symbolic apple. Incidentally, Eve has gained a lot of empathy in some circles for having been cast in the role of weak, wily feminine, just as another mother symbol, Mary, has been whitewashed of all of her humanity.

Actually, Eve and Mary each play a very important role mythologically, opening the possibility for a new kind of consciousness that the masculine alone would not allow. Archetypally, the feminine is the voice of accommodation and containment, the inclusive voice of yes, so only Eve and Mary would be capable of saying yes to housing God and yes to becoming conscious. As one might guess, the masculine is usually the exclusionary voice of no, the voice of the sword and the lance, of discernment and definition. We need the archetypal energy of both the feminine and masculine voices, and Jesus Christ as a symbol of the Self shows us a way to access each of these resources with an appropriate measure of balance and timing.

The second consequence of becoming conscious is that you became aware of death. Every living organism will die, but as far as we know, human beings are the only creatures with a consciousness of death.

What makes us crazy is that one, we're part of a mystery we don't understand, and two, we're hardwired for survival. We are semiconscious of a source that we came from, and we are seeking that source as a resource for our journey. We have all kinds of fantasies and projections about reconnecting to this source. One reason that Christianity has resonated for so many people, for so many centuries, is that it "speaks the language of human emotions," to quote Pagels's wonderfully poetic description once again, by addressing our deepest fear—the fear of death—and promising us a way to overcome our mortality.

We can ask, "Is life a problem to be solved or a mystery to be experienced?" When we are able to hold the paradox consciously, we can answer, "Both." We can integrate the opposites, which tell us that according to Proposition A, any postgrave existence is an illusion created by the ego to assuage its anxiety about disappearing, while on the other hand, Proposition B tells us that the illusion of life after death is archetypal, implanted in us from the beginning. If we take this second proposition, we can say that through death we come to a higher consciousness or knowing.

The truth is that the ego, which is about the size of a cork bobbing on the sea compared to the vast unconscious, just doesn't know very much. The quantum physicists are now saying that we never had it right with our concept of three dimensions in time and space, and that there are likely as many as seven or eight dimensions. Just think about that. Right now, we are probably existing in four or five dimensions that we are not even conscious of. So, in the end, I suspect there is a kind of postgrave existence where we will go into different dimensions that we can't even conceptualize with our limited human knowledge. That's kind of my hope and expectation, that we will enter into a new realm of higher consciousness. I certainly hope I don't go to a literal heaven to spend eternity with the fundamentalists!

In the Jungian viewpoint, evil is seen as an important element in the dynamic process of becoming conscious. The tension between good and evil as paired opposites continually forces us to decide, which affirms our lives and causes us to grow. If we don't have to decide, then we never really live. The root of *decide* means "to kill or die," helping us to see that every decision is both death dealing and life giving. The ability to decide is a large part of this grace and burden of being human. We should be so grateful that we get to decide, but for many of us, making a decision is such an anxiety-producing task, a responsibility of such consequence, that we would like to abdicate that responsibility to somebody else, which is the dynamic behind the growing wave of fundamentalism in this ever more complex world.

While deciding can be difficult, Jung said that psychologically it is very important to be able to decide, to put into motion the dynamic of good and evil. While the source of good and evil may be somewhat of a mystery, if it is not indeed the Creator, we do know a lot about the nature of good and evil psychologically. The goal of good is wholeness, and the goal of evil is nothingness. The process of the good is integration, and the process of evil is dis-integration.

While we can define good and evil, we can't always separate them. In other words, there are many actions and events that are both simultaneously, paradoxically, good and evil. In fact, this dual nature may apply to the majority of actions and events. This is an idea that is crazy making for us with our Western minds and our masculine-dominated either/or consciousness, but we can't get to our next level of development until we hold that paradox consciously. With its better balance of the masculine and feminine, the Eastern mind is much more adept at grasping the yin-and-yang nature of this duality.

I have 30 years of experience in helping people and observing their processes, and I've seen countless times how particular actions and decisions in people's lives were both integrating and disintegrating—both good and evil—at the same time. Many times, the worst thing that can ever happen in life is also the best thing that could happen. It's a paradox—something can be simultaneously integrative and disintegrative. Illness, divorce, job loss, and other life events are disintegrative times when something is being torn apart and broken down. At the same time, something new is emerging and is being integrated toward wholeness.

Coming to consciousness about this paradox is what Jung called the transcendent function, in the sense that we are creating something new and coming to a new level. We hold two opposites consciously until they are integrated, and we come to a higher consciousness, which is the ability to ask, "Is that what I chose to do, or is it that what chose me?"

We can say that an experience was at the same time both destructive and constructive, both evil and good. And because of our consciousness of this paradox, we are able to take the totality of our experience and from it make something new that never existed before. This is what we would call resurrectional. From our worldview as Christians, can we possibly see that Jesus's death was both disintegrating and integrating at the same time?

*Resurrection* means coming to transcendence or to a new consciousness that is able to take that act of simultaneous dis-integration and re-integration to a new level of consciousness that is characterized by maturity, commitment to life, meaning, and a thousand other things. In short, it is to be reborn into the kingdom of God.

Once again, this is a process the ego would love to romanticize, but it is a difficult process, because you have to do it consciously and without judgment, something that's almost impossible in our culture. We say that judgment is the enemy of analysis, for when something is judged it is labeled, compartmentalized, and filed away, and thus we can find an excuse to refuse the hard work of analysis. We'd rather say, "That was horrible!" "That was a bad thing." "A sin." And when we do so, we slam shut the door to an opportunity for growth in consciousness. We would be better off it we asked, "How did I get here? Where is this leading? How can I be transformed by this? How can I do as the alchemists attempted, and take this *prima materia* (shit) and turn it into gold?" We should be able to turn shit into gold simultaneously. After all, it's fertilizer.

I've said before in a thousand places that to be conscious is apparently a new thing for humans. We're just not very good at it. We have this hubris that we've evolved in our consciousness, but we can test just how far we've evolved by looking at our behavior, which is still too often marred by primitive impulses such as our reptilian territoriality. All we need for confirmation of that is to turn on the news.

If we look at infants, we can see that it almost looks as if consciousness is not natural for human beings. It's not something they can sustain for very long periods of time before disintegrating into anxiety and panic, needing the soothing and containment that the maternal archetype provides. Part of our maturation process is developing the ability to sustain consciousness for longer periods of time. Even when we reach chronological maturity, we have trouble sustaining consciousness for 18 hours at a time, and even during that 18 hours, we go into altered states of consciousness all day long.

Further, human consciousness is divided by this great ambiguity. We don't always know what's right or wrong, good or bad, healthy or unhealthy. We have this unlimited freedom of will informed by very limited information, hence we are always reexamining our decisions in retrospect and saying, "At the time, it seemed like the right thing to do."

It appears that we have a culture predominantly committed to remaining unconscious. We shy away from the rigorous hard work of becoming conscious, despite our cultural ego identification with hard work, despite the Puritan work ethic that has been ingrained in us by our American religion, the same centuries-old work ethic that keeps us as tied to our cell phones and Blackberries as our forefathers were strapped to their plows.

Among all the deaths we experience, the biological death is probably the least challenging. Everybody seems to be able to do that. But the death of the ego, which must be accomplished if the Self is to dwell in the kingdom of God, is a very difficult one. It's an ego-cide we must consciously de-cide to commit, for the ego is that organ of consciousness that creates the illusion of security through structure, but the structure is what prevents us from deciding and ultimately from living.

Actually, what's needed is not so much a death for the ego as a demotion, but the ego in its self-centered insecurity sees any kind of change as life threatening. The irony is that once the ego relinquishes its power, it retains a vitally important place in the psyche. We must have strong egos in order to give them up, and there's a difference between a strong ego and a big ego. A big, inflated ego is an obvious compensation for an inferiority complex. In the kingdom within, the ego is not the king; that is the proper role of the Self. The ego's appropriate place is to serve as an organ of consciousness, of discernment and identity. But the ultimate discerner of one's true vocation is the Self, and how the Self gets constellated into the world in creative, dynamic, and evolving modes of consciousness.

Living for the Self means becoming authentic and autonomous, and there are great risks inherent in this process. There is no better example of this than Christ himself. Institutions and power structures get suspicious about autonomy, because autonomy can lead to anarchy. The fear is that autonomy can be overtaken by ego as inflated hubris, which generally leads to disintegration or evil. It's an important warning that religions have long cautioned us about, but it is no reason to avoid the task of becoming conscious and autonomous. It's also true that autonomy has a natural companion, responsibility, and some of the most responsible people I know are those who are authentically autonomous. It's the people who are stuck in unconsciousness, who are suffering and don't know any other way to get out, who act violent and sociopathic.

In the kingdom of God or the kingdom within, Jesus had in mind an intensely personal state of being, potentially open to all people, but to which only a few will be conscious enough to respond to the calling. Those who enter the kingdom will have to shed their masks and confront their inner enemies. They will embrace a creative ethic founded on conscious awareness of the Self. The road to the kingdom will be an inner road, a way of the soul. Nothing can be excluded that belongs to our wholeness, not even those parts of us that we have despised all our lives, which we are now called to embrace and integrate.

Many theologians and psychologists have tried to view the Christian myth through a new lens, to view it as a myth with great power and efficacy for meaning, wholeness, and psychological health. Critics will say that this is an attempt to psychologize Christianity. Adherents will say it's opening up and revitalizing the religion. In the end, each one of us gets to choose and decide. The only tragedy is using this myth as an authoritarian fear tactic to keep people subordinate and infantilized. To me, that is the real evil.

## CHAPTER 9

# FINDING A HEALTHY SPIRITUALITY AND ENCOUNTERING THE TRANSCENDENT IN EVERYDAY LIFE

Two opposing heresies have always coexisted in religious life, but the split has never been more dramatic than in recent times.

To begin taking away the judgment and condemnation that has come to be associated with the word *heresy*, we can look at its origin, the Greek word *hairesis*, meaning a choice of beliefs. Like political victors who enjoy the privilege of writing their own version of history, the dominant religious structure has had the power to declare which beliefs are orthodox (meaning "straight thinking") and which are heretical. In the final analysis, whether a belief is heretical or not boils down to point of view. The Roman Catholic Church labeled Protestantism as heresy, while many Protestants returned the favor by calling Catholicism the Great Apostasy.

For our discussion, the heresies are found in the two extremes of viewing religion as literal fact or nonrational fiction. In the Jungian worldview, the assumption is that sacred stories, symbols, and the other contents of religion are mythological, which leads us to a different way of treating this material than if it were historical, sociological, or political. Looking at religious material from a mythological viewpoint, we are led to ask, "What are the spiritual, psychological, and archetypal truths to be found in these sacred stories and symbols?" And also, "What are the implications for the psyche, which is to say our inner world?"

With the two splits, however, the tremendous mythological wealth of religion falls into either one of two great chasms. On the one hand, there are the literalists, who would concretize the stories and the symbols, to say, "The

Bible says it, I believe it, that settles it." Which seems to me to be heretical, because it trivializes the substantial gift of our transpersonal heritage.

This leads to a great irony, where the very true believers who reject the opposite heresy—rationalism—are frequently seduced into the very rationalistic position of trying to prove mythological material as literal fact. The very idea that someone would want to try to prove that in year 1573 B.C. a child was swallowed by a great fish in the Indian Ocean, and three days later, he was spit out and lived to tell the story! In *God on Your Own*, the former monk Joseph Dispenza describes the "tyranny of the literal" as "terribly limiting, especially when we are looking for spiritual truths."[1]

Concerning the literalness of stories such as that of the virgin birth, the theologian Frederick Buechner reminds us that we shouldn't confuse gynecology with theology. And it bears repeating what Jung said about discerning the difference between physical fact and spiritual truth. The other heresy is the reductionist viewpoint, which seeks to reduce a sacred story back to some scientific basis in order to answer questions such as, "Is this possible? Was this true? Could it have actually happened?" And then if a story doesn't hold up to contemporary scientific methodology or theories, it must be thrown out as make-believe.

It's interesting to me that each of these extremes is interested in proving itself to the other side, or disproving as it were. This is what Campbell called the "baby in the bathwater" problem of mythological material. The medium is the bathwater, and truth is the baby, but if the medium is out-of-date cosmologically, the reductionists want to throw it out, so that the living baby is lost along with what is viewed as stagnant water. If a story doesn't square with our scientific knowledge, if it doesn't fit the template of modern scientific consensus, then it must be dismissed.

Those of us who are interested in mythology believe that the myth is the container for the truth of what it means to be human, and that this truth is archetypal, meaning that it fits into the transpersonal collective consciousness in all times and all places. The reason the myths get passed along from generation to generation is that they carry the truth. The consensus may change from generation to generation, but the truth does not. Take the creation story of Adam and Eve. This myth doesn't fit into what scientific knowledge tells us about evolution and the origin of the human race, but it does provide a parable for understanding how the human race came to exist on an incredibly fecund planet, and on another level it informs us about the cost of becoming conscious.

As one who has stood up and talked publicly about religion for 25 years, I have been critiqued by both extremes. And I understand where my critics are coming from, for I have both a fundamentalist preacher and a rational scientist living inside of me. There are times I would love to have something for once in my life that is absolutely true and concrete, just the way the Bible says it. Another part of me would like to say, "Maybe the evolutionary psychologists are right when they say that our strongest instinct is survival, and that religion and myths have come into being to help us get though this."

If we are going to be good twenty-first-century theologians, it's important not to be seduced by either side, although sometimes it's very difficult to live in the middle of them. We must live the paradox and recognize that two things can be true at once, that we are merely organisms most interested in survival, and that each of us carries a holy, divine vocation within us. Are we human, or are we divine? The answer to each is yes, and that ambivalence creates a split, creating the confusion and anxiety that comes out of not knowing.

Continuing to work through Campbell's four functions of myth, another function is mythology's ability to help us access the mystical realm, to attach us to that part of the human experience that is beyond the reach of our consciousness. The myth gives us a sense there is something transcendent among us, only a short distance from our experience. Another function is cosmological, helping us formulate a response to the questions, "Where did we come from? What are we here for? Where are we going?" Myth helps us answer these questions, setting up a cosmology to explain creation. All cultures have had creation stories, and there is always a kind of chauvinism which says, "Our creation story makes sense and yours is ridiculous."

In one of my favorite anecdotes, given by Stephen Hawking in *A Brief History of Time*, Bertrand Russell is given credit for recounting one very sophisticated theory of creation. Russell was lecturing on evolution, and at the end of the lecture, a woman stood up and said, "You're a brilliant young man, Dr. Russell, but you've got it wrong. The world is a plate that is resting on the back of a giant tortoise." He then said, "But my good lady, on what does that turtle rest?" To which the woman responded, with the tinge of impatience that comes from having to state the obvious, "Dr. Russell, it's turtles all the way down!" For her, the turtle creation story must have resonated!

The beautiful novel *Life of Pi* begins with the line, "I am going to tell you a story that will make you believe in God," and the narrator goes on to recount the wondrous tale of a young boy adrift on the ocean in a lifeboat, with animals including a tiger and a hyena representing the full spectrum of humanity's capacity for good and evil. Before the narrator wakes up in a hospital, with two no-nonsense Japanese insurance adjusters standing over him, his adventures include washing up on a mystical island that turns out to be a floating mass of seaweed. At the end, he asks which story we prefer—the one filled with symbolism, wonder, and meaning, or the kind of dry report that only an insurance executive could love?

The mythological formula is an attempt to apply what we do know to what we don't know, to try and bridge the gap between the two. As we evolve in our collective consciousness and consensus reality, many times the mythological structure that was once appropriate for a particular time and place may no longer work in the present, so we must find and salvage the truth of that sacred story amid the anachronistic supporting details. We can analyze many creation stories and discern similar things being said, and that is what we would call the archetypal content. If we throw the baby (the truth) out with the bathwater (the mythological container or medium), then we miss a great opportunity to understand ourselves and human nature.

It is encouraging to me that this idea of drinking from the well of symbol and myth seems to be the emerging religious viewpoint. We have begun to develop a postmodern understanding that we have for too long ignored the nonrational and nonmaterial in favor of the rational and material, resulting in this painful split between the dueling heresies of literalism and scientific reductionism. Rather than remain satisfied with the dry canals of literalism and rationalism, we have become thirsty for the living water of symbol and myth, which soothes the soul rather than assuages ego anxiety.

Jung was very prophetic when he said that mankind was entering a New Age where we would reclaim the value of symbol and myth, and recognize the value of the collective and personal unconscious. Jung gave us that wonderful quotation that around the year 1500, when the universe was moving from the age of Pisces to the age of Aquarius, that God fell out of the heavens and into human consciousness. Only this far in retrospect can we see that the sixteenth century marked the beginning of modernity, a New Age characterized by the evolution of the individual out of the collective. Up until this time, the individual identity had been subordinated to the family, tribe, or religion. We got our identity from an external source, but this new evolution in human consciousness marked the beginning of what Jung called individuation. He posited that the divine was to be rediscovered, existentially, in the psyche of every human being, in the wisdom of the inner Self.

When Jung called individuation the new God image for the New Age, he meant that there is a *vox deo*, or "voice of god," and an *imago dei*, or "god image," in each human being, which is essentially what the Gnostics had been saying all along. Jung called for a return to Gnostic sense of God as an inner and directing spirit, and said there is something divine about the human enterprise. He said that each individual has the moral obligation and the divine opportunity to become whole, and that this was the new holy and sacred vocation, to be undertaken with the help of symbols and sacred stories as resources.

The dawn of new ages and the emergence of paradigm shifts occur at a glacial pace, although in retrospect, the transitions can seem much more defined. During the sixteenth century, mankind pretty much went with the Cartesian split of "I think, therefore I am," which would overemphasize the logical and the masculine for the next 500 years. It has taken us half a millennium to get to where we are today, where we have begun to evolve to a collective consciousness that is ready to embrace the New Age and its counterbalancing emphasis on the feminine and mystical elements of our nature.

I have seen this paradigm shift all over the country, in small but sincere groups of people who are interested in rescuing not only Christianity from the twin heresies of literalism and rationalism, but other myths as well, including the Jewish, Hindu, and Buddhist traditions. These seekers want to recover the sacred stories and symbolic content of these great mythological systems and to revision this content as guidelines for what it means to be a healthy human being in the twenty-first century.

We have even seen this paradigm shift in the mental health field. When I started out as a young priest, it was clear that the mental health tradition considered spirituality or religion as a form of neurosis, especially when they were exhibited with any degree of zealousness. Now, so-called spiritual therapy is a widely accepted form of counseling—another sign that we have entered a New Age. We are at the very front end of this age, and it is by far not the predominant way of thinking in our current society, but a fundamental paradigm shift is indeed under way, and there is no putting the genie back in the bottle.

The emergence of the New Age is a major contributing factor to the rise in fundamentalist religious beliefs, for it further adds to the radical pluralism that is running throughout the world today. This state of flux, while exhilarating to some, only increases the anxiety already felt by many who are looking to the authority structures for clear, black-and-white answers. In this New Age, it is very possible to be a person of faith and belief and yet be critical of literal interpretations of biblical accounts. This is a paradox that offers a very liberating third way or middle road between the rocky cliffs of either literalism or reductionism, but for many, the paradox is just too difficult to hold consciously, and many run to find comfort in the dead certainty of either extreme.

We can see a readiness to embrace the New Age in the widespread popular interest in recent discoveries such as the Gnostic Gospels and the Gospel of Judas, which offer divergent viewpoints from the old doctrinal orthodoxy. We see further evidence of this paradigm shift in the popular retellings of old legends, such as the runaway bestseller, *The Da Vinci Code*.

It has been a recurring and consistent pattern throughout human history that legends arise from the collective unconscious and begin to gain a foothold in consciousness when myths become unbalanced. It is the nature of nature to seek balance, so legends come into being to provide a counterbalance when myths have strayed too far to one side or another. So if we canonize an interpretation of the myth that says Jesus never had sex or sexual thoughts, and repress any interpretation to the contrary, it is inevitable that this one-sided pureness, which denies the human factor in the human-divine paradox that is Jesus Christ, will give rise to legends such as the one about Christ having married Mary Magdalene and raised a family in France. I'm certain that Dan Brown had no idea of what he had gotten a hold of when he wrote *The Da Vinci Code*, but he hit a nerve in the collective consciousness, and his book took off like Mercury. He didn't invent anything or add anything new to legends that had been circulating for centuries, but he did do a masterful job of weaving these tales together with a spellbinding counternarrative to the prevailing, unbalanced myth.

The same dynamic is found in the legend of the Black Madonna, which religious scholars suggest has grown out of pre-Christian earth goddess traditions. With her dark skin suggesting earthiness and fertility, the Black Madonna offers a counterpoint to the image of the pristine, lily-white Virgin Mary, who has been sanitized of all her humanity. These and other legends come back to show us that we may become unbalanced at any point in our individual and collective lives. We can become so unbalanced that we deny our humanity at one extreme, or that we deny our divinity at the other. The legends tell us that we need to hold the paradox of the opposites consciously, so that we may live the full spectrum of our birthright, which is to be both human and divine simultaneously.

Clearly, the old way of being in the church doesn't work for many people, so what does work for this growing community of seekers? What would a healthy spirituality for the twenty-first century look like, as if we could even begin to come up with a definitive answer to that vitally important question? I don't have any idealized or neurotic viewpoint that I am the authority on what healthy spirituality is. My concern is that you begin to claim your own authority about what a healthy spirituality is and no longer continue to look outside yourself for an answer to such a substantial, important, deep, and meaningful question.

I do hope that I can address the questions in a way that might help resonate something that will come into your own consciousness and help you answer the questions for yourself. I have no interest in providing a structure or set of rules that would just replace the old ones I have encouraged you to throw away. If I could bequeath anything about what constitutes a healthy spirituality, I would say that one, it is its own authority, and two, it is experiential.

On authority, a mature spirituality means that I do not look outside myself any longer for somebody to take care of me. I look for guides and I look for companions, but I don't look for external authorities. I become conscious of the projections I have made onto religious structures, and even God images, to take care of me, because the dark side of the mother means that she will infantilize you and keep you dependent, and the dark side of the father brings shame, punishment, and exclusion.

I'm not saying that we don't have guides or road maps, or that we don't look for help to those who are a chapter or two ahead of us. It is part of being human to look for guides and mentors who will help us develop our own authority. Keep in mind that any authority worth his salt will empower you to become your own authority, rather than keeping you dependent and infantilizing you. It seems to me that the world is divided into searchers and saluters. Searchers being those who seek the truth on their own terms, and saluters being those who constitute and perpetuate the status quo. I don't know why people are different—perhaps woundedness has a lot to do with it—but for me, all of my mentors have always been searchers. Ultimately, you and I must each decide what is to be our spirituality, using our incumbent experience and authority as resources.

What do we mean by experiential? Foremost, that God is an experience, not a concept. Jung said that each of us has a divine spark within us, allowing us an immediate experience of God. By immediate, he meant personal and intimate, in the sense that it happens to me and to you, not in the sense of America's need for instant gratification. He thought the transcendent was an immanent presence, a state of being in which thinking and feeling are unified and grounded, in a sense of one's immediate participation in the divine. Jung wrote upon having a breakthrough experience, "Suddenly, I understood that God was for me at least one of the most certain and immediate experiences of life." We need to experience God for ourselves, rather than looking to a traditional authoritarian interpretation of the symbols and sacred stories. We can experience the divine using the resources of religion as our guiding wisdom and accepting at the outset that we can't do it without making mistakes or having regressive moments.

Once again, we have a paradox: is living in the kingdom of God an inner or outer experience? The answer is both. It seems to me that when the inner world and outer world are indistinguishable, those moments are holy. When I don't know whether I'm in the inner or outer world, and when it feels irrelevant to even consider the question, then I am in the kingdom of God, the kingdom within, the Dao, or the golden world.

Paul Tillich says, "mystery is reason driven beyond itself, experienced objectively as miracle, and subjectively as ecstasy."[2] In many seminars and lectures, I've asked people to share with me their mystical experience or miraculous moment, and it is fascinating and wonderful to see that ordinary people have extraordinary things happen to them, most profoundly and most simply. My experience is no different than yours in that it just takes certain eyes to see and ears to hear, and all of a sudden things are opened up.

Interestingly enough, when I've asked people if they have ever had a religious or miraculous experience, a high percentage of times, it's around birth and death, those two great extremes that are the same. For me, the most miraculous events that I have ever experienced were the births of my two sons and my grandson. I was present for all, and moments of transcendence and transformation were those. I've written some very mediocre poetry, I've given some good lectures, I've analyzed some great people, but the best thing I have ever done was birth two sons and raise them.

I'm generally opposed to making lists, but I'm going to offer one as an ending to this book. I think lists are probably a pretty good pedagogical trick, but I have usually resisted them, partly because every Saturday in the *Houston Chronicle*'s religion page, many of the advertisements for local churches include the titles of the sermons planned for the next day, and too often the title involves a trite list. (My all-time favorite sermon title is still, "Ten Top Tips for Tip Top Christians.")

Nonetheless, I want to end with seven ways we have traditionally experienced God and the transrational realm. Both are beyond knowing and naming, but we can find them in ways that include nature, art and creativity, ritual process, relationships, suffering, our bodies, and dreams.

## NATURE

When you and I look at a tree, a flower, or anything in nature, we are the universe looking at its handiwork, said the Unitarian Universalist minister Greta Crosby. We are the eye of God looking upon creation, and God depends upon our conscious awareness to be able to see.

Thomas Cahill recounts the many gifts the ancient Hibernians offered humankind, but which we have lost or refused. Chief among these was an attitude of mysticism, which viewed the body and all the world as holy. In the poem, *Saint Patrick's Breastplate* (described by Cahill as "entirely un-Augustinian in feeling"), we find humankind's "first ringing assertion that the universe itself as the Great Sacrament, magically designed by its loving Creator to bless and succor human beings."[3]

Oh, but what a sad time it is to be human, in an age where we have never been so separated from nature, the cathedral of the world. She is our mother, and we know so little about her any longer, living in our glass and concrete world. The transcendent comes screaming into the world through nature. As the Sierra Club founder John Muir said, "The clearest way into the Universe is through a forest wilderness."

Unfortunately, we've cut down most of the forests, and with our workaholic, overscheduled lives, we can hardly find the resolve to get into our car and drive down the freeway until we come to nearest forest remnant. Even what passes for celebrating nature in our competitive, consumer-obsessed culture still has more of the feeling of conquering or subduing her, as the TV commercials urge us to "Just do it" or gas up our four-wheel-drive SUVs and get out there.

We have been poor stewards over this earth we've been given dominion over, exploiting her resources and denying the mounting evidence that we are destroying her. For many years now, she has been offering us clues about the catastrophic climate change we are causing, yet we have ignored them, nowhere more so than in this country, where we have refused to participate in global-warming treaties, fearing that helping save the earth might harm the economy we idolize. To paraphrase Luke, what profiteth a country to gain a few points on its stock exchange, only to lose the world? This is one instance where literalism would be appropriate. Nature is our mother and she nurtures us, but we are antagonizing her into showing us a very dark and negative side—one that will give new meaning to the old saying, "Hell hath no fury like a woman scorned."

But in the here and now, if we can only be truly present, there is still plenty of opportunity to encounter the transcendent in nature.

We can find much of life's sweetness in nature, not to mention its wonder. In his biography, Barack Obama recalls how his mother shared with him an enduring sense of wonder and reverence for life, and how she found unending joy in its mystery and even its strangeness. He tells of how she would sometimes wake him in the middle of night so he could join her in admiring a particularly spectacular moon, or how she would have him close his eyes and listen to the rustle of autumn leaves as they walked together at twilight. A human mother helping her child to connect with the archetypal mother— now that is positive mothering.

It has always been interesting to me when capitalistic, workaholic males who compete and defeat in the warrior archetype arrive at some place of success in our society—at least success measured by money—the first thing they do is buy a house in the country. They want to get back to the earth. No matter how complex or cutoff we become, we still know instinctively that nature is the only mother who can sooth our savaged souls, inviting us to walk beside still waters and graze in green pastures.

The Creator wants us to experience the healing and restorative aspects of nature. The Episcopal priest Barbara Brown Taylor writes of how Jesus often encouraged the disciples to get away for a little while, to find a quiet place to rest. Even amid crowds of hungry people—or customers—the invitation to rest still stands. "The distinct possibility that what God wants from me is not a worn-out, empty sack of myself, but my full and whole humanity...was a huge discovery for me," Taylor said in an interview.

Many years before it became a truism in our wired and tired society, the jazz singer Nena Simone said, "You can use up everything you got giving everybody everything they want." To recharge and replenish everything we've got, there are few resources better than Mother Nature.

How can we reconnect with nature, when we have so long blocked ourselves off from her? The Japanese Zen poet Masahide tells us,

Barn's burnt down—
now
I can see the moon.

What barns have we constructed that keep us from seeing nature, our mother? What is it that will ignite the flame that will burn down the boxes we have created that keep us from seeing the Truth in her? She is in nature and she is available to us, for those of us who have the eyes to see and the ears to hear, who are willing to slow down and become pedestrian mystics, so that we can walk softly and see the heaven that lies about us and open ourselves to a clearer vision.

Nature is available to us in the most simple and immediate places: our gardens, our backyards, our neighborhood parks. What about that wildflower, too often dismissed as a weed, growing out of the crack in the concrete, reminding us of how the Buddhists find transcendence in the image of a lotus pushing its dazzling bloom up out of the muck of a stagnant pond? The garden, of course, is where life emanates, where it all began, as our myth tells us.

Who among us regularly takes the time to perceive that the transcendent is available to us in our everyday, quotidian world? It is there before us. God is not devious, but God is subtle, according to Albert Einstein. "My religion consists of a humble admiration of the illimitable superior spirit who reveals himself in the slight details we are able to perceive with our frail and feeble mind," said the modest genius.

The Creator has woven the Creator's self into all of creation, and into every creature, yet we all hide behind the barn, wondering where we will ever find the truth. We just can't see the truth, because of all of these structures we've built—ego defenses, distractions, repressions, suppressions, projections, and on and on. They are all barns, artificial structures created to protect us, and yet they do not even fulfill that role. We had the illusion in the first half of life that these structures were keeping us alive, but in the second half of life, they are keeping us from living. If we can only burn the barns down, we would be able to see the moon.

## CREATIVITY

The Creator has implanted the Creator's self into creation and into every creature, and our celebration and response to that is creativity. Creativity is a significant part of what makes us fully human, as Margaret Atwood notes with her observation that the dividing line between us and our evolutionary ancestors seems to be around the time we began making art. Those cave paintings and burial rituals were so much more than attempts to leave behind documentary records of what had been experienced. They were among the first attempts by conscious beings to bridge the gaps between what they observed in one realm and what they believed had happened—or would happen—in another, more mysterious dimension. Possessing instincts far superior to those we possess today, our ancestors had the vague but undeniable idea that this realm was as much of a reality as the primordial world that surrounded them.

I recently overheard a conversation at the Museum of Fine Arts in Houston, among three folks standing around a large abstract modern painting. One guy started off by commenting that the painting looked like some Sheetrock he had recently repaired and wondered how it could be called art. The second friend—no doubt a little more culturally sophisticated—talked about how the abstract artist plunges into the blank canvas with a single mark or brushstroke, surrendering herself to the creative process without having any idea of where it will ultimately take her. The third, silent until now, said, "It's kind of like the Creator is creating itself through you."

That was as good an explanation as I have ever heard for creativity, all from one little overheard conversation that touched on creativity, as well as doubt, faith, mystery, and the journey. The fruit of our creativity doesn't have to hang on a museum wall to be seen by critics, or to be published or purchased. If it expresses the joy of the human experience for no one but the creator, then it is worthwhile.

Of all the souls in the universe, says Plato, we're the most fortunate, because we've been invited into the human experience. We're really not human beings trying to become spiritual, we're spiritual beings trying to become human. We do that by having the human experience, and creativity is so much a part of it. Creativity can be dancing by yourself in the kitchen to Patsy Cline. Writing a piece of doggerel while you sit waiting for the next plane. Doodling on a pad while you talk on the phone. It's all creativity. It's expressive and available, whether we dance it, sing it, draw it, write it, or rhyme it. Find the creativity, and you'll find yourself experiencing the mystical presence of the transcendent in the most simple and available way.

I love the human being's ability to sit and watch a garden for a cycle of seasons and see all of human nature revealed. You can sit in your own backyard and watch a tree in the cycle of its seasons revealing something of the nature of what it means to be human, from autumn's necessary death to springtime's resurrection. To see, as Eliot saw, that April is the cruelest month of the year, when that knuckled bud is experiencing the trauma of birth and coming back again with blossom and bloom.

To sit in a chair and watch a tree for a cycle of seasons is a creative act of nature and creativity. Even further is to realize that we are sitting in a chair, looking at a tree, mirroring a human being in a cycle of seasons, and to realize that we are sitting in a chair made of trees, in a house of trees, warming ourselves from the shard and the bark from the trunk of a tree, reading a book made from trees about trees. I like human beings and their ability to integrate nature and creativity!

Why do we not joyously celebrate the Creator by expressing the Creator's presence within us through creativity? What's the barn that needs to be burnt in order for us to see that? What are those fears, those narcissistic fears that keep us from expressing the joys of being alive and being human? This being human is a time-limited experience, after all. Here is the meantime, the in-between time, why do we sit frozen fearfully?

I remember my piano teacher growing up in Oklahoma. She tolerated me for about six months, though she made it clear to my mother and father that I would have another calling. She did say something memorable, though. One day she told me, "Pittman, when you play the piano, don't worry about making mistakes. That's how you learn to play." I may have been an unteachable piano student, but I have never forgotten her most valuable lesson: there are no mistakes. Mistakes are only processes of perfecting the art of being. All of our mistakes are the very substance from which we make soul. The only nutriment of the soul is experience, and some of the most nourishing experiences are those that don't work for us.

As Johnson once told me, if we take two steps forward and one step back, we're making progress, for life is not a linear process. If we take two steps forward and three steps back, then we're going the wrong direction. So those experiences that don't work out as we'd like are not mistakes, but rather helpful signs that we are not headed in the right direction.

After my piano lessons in Drumright came the dance lessons—my parents were determined to make a cultured young man out of me. A dance teacher from the Arthur Murray studio in Tulsa would come into town for the day, setting up her Motorola record player in the American Legion hall. She would lay these cutout footprints down on the floor, providing a visual map to the mystery of the waltz, and each of us awkward youngsters was forced to follow the preordained footsteps. Even then, dancing with a girl too tall for me, I knew this wasn't dancing, at least not the kind I wanted to do. In dancing, as in life, you cannot follow the footprints on the floor. You have to throw them away and dance to your own creativity.

## RITUAL PROCESS

The rituals that we invent for ourselves, or which have been invented for us, put us in a context in which we might experience the transcendent. Our rituals can be as formal as worship and attendance at temple, church, ashram, or mosque. As a Christian and a priest of the church, I live my life between baptism and Eucharist, and those ritual processes of sacrament and the symbolic life are very important and efficacious. They work even if we are not conscious of their role as containers for our symbols, myths, and mysteries, yet they are much more powerful if we approach them with that consciousness. As a friend of mine said, how much you get from the well depends on the size of your bucket, a metaphor for the depth and understanding we bring to ritual process. The same friend also said he still gets a buzz out of the Eucharist, even after decades of rehearsal.

But our sacred rites are not the only meaningful rituals in our lives. There is a ritual process that we may experience every morning, involving meditation and prayer, opening ourself to the possibility that we might get the barn out of the way just enough to see the moon. We can draw circles on the floor, light candles, and meditate at home on a rug or in the garden. The most profound symbols are the most elementary symbols, and we all have ready access to these in water, light, wind, and earth.

And what about that morning ritual in the bathroom, where we enjoy that sacred space of privacy for elimination, adornment, and cleansing? These water rituals are wonderful in providing a daily cleansing act with baptismal efficacy.

We don't have to leave our own homes to experience the sacred. Why not have the kind of consciousness and the eyes to see that the places where we live are sacred, that even our most mundane, perfunctory activities can be sacramental if undertaken with the right kind of reverent awareness? Our homes are sanctuaries alive with possibilities for experiencing the transcendent. God is available wherever we are, and there's a certain autonomy of God, who appears in the most interesting and unexpected places.

There is also a ritual process of returning to the unconscious every night, where we go back into the maternal womb of darkness, with the simple act of going to sleep with a cool glass of water, a warm bed, and a feeling of gratitude that the transcendent is available every night. We will awaken refreshed and renewed, brought back every morning to a new life that has never been before and will never be again. We can begin our ritual process for the day by thanking God that there's a floor when we pull out of bed, providing us with a sense of foundation and trust that today, like every day, will be worthwhile.

Johnson likens the introspection of personal ritual process to a kind of "inner incest" that helps us build soul and grow in consciousness. "When you go off to meditate or simply refresh yourself after work or community, you are mating with yourself. One stream of energy is being introduced to another stream of energy, and their fusion produces an offspring."[4]

So ritual process then is not just at the ashram or the monastery or the cathedral, but it's in our own homes and our own lives, found in the daily, quotidian routines that can become our own personal ritual process, calling us to a clearer vision wherein we see the heaven that lies about us, and that God is as near as hands and feet. We must always resist the possibility that our rituals and traditions can become, as the author Barbara Tober put it, group efforts to keep the unexpected from happening. As long as we approach our personal and collective rituals with the right kind of consciousness, they can provide a luminous framework that supports our spiritual quest, at the same time allowing the transcendent to shine through as clearly as the sun shines through a structure as formal as a rose window or as ephemeral as a spider's web.

## LOVE

I am told that you can tell how much importance a culture places on something by the number of words it has for it. The Inuit have 52 words for snow; we have 1. Obviously, being able to express the many nuances of snow is much more important to the survival of the Inuit culture than ours. But what about love? What does it say about our culture that we only have one word for love? What about the many forms of love, such as love for God, spouses, children, siblings, and everything for which we feel connection? Other cultures, such as the Hindus, have a wealth of words to convey very precise and specialized meanings for love. There is even a Hindi word for the love you feel for your horse.

In our culture, we have such a paltry, limited understanding of love, though the Greeks have helped us a little, contributing words and roots such as *Eros, agape,* and *philia.* Most of us have been seduced into believing that the truest, deepest love we can aspire to is the kind of cardboard love hawked by Hallmark or the celluloid love sold by Hollywood. Eros, once such a substantial mover of human emotions, has been reduced to a cardboard Cupid, mailed every February and then forgotten in a drawer.

The kind of love we've all but lost is the love that puts us face to face with the transcendent. It is the love that the philosopher and Hasidic theologian Martin Buber talks about in *I and Thou.* It is agape, the unsentimental, substantial love of a subject for a subject (as opposed to an object), and it is so strong that one subject is willing to give itself up for the other.

Agape is that love that lets be, not in the apathetic sense, but in the empowering sense of allowing one to be and become that which they were created to be. And to support that, rather than bind it up with predetermined notions of what it means for all human beings to be human. It means having enough love to witness a lifetime of time-lapsed photographs as the beloved evolves into that special, unique creature that they were created to be, as God conceived of them at their conception. The ability to let it be and to behold the uniqueness of every human being is the deepest form of love.

Love is not just about that warm feeling. Love is about that substantial connection that empowers another to be what they were created to be. Love in this sense is where we see the Creator in the creature. After all, what we seek in love is the experience of the transcendent in the Other, the transpersonal self that we experience in the Other.

I love the Greek word *perichoresis,* which means "to dance around." Perichoretic love is the love that dances around and contains and empowers.

Those who dwell in love dance around the transcendent experience that offers meaning, purpose, and transformation. It's available, but we are so heavily defended against it that we rarely experience it.

Years ago, a friend of mine named Charles was an inner-city priest in Louisville. One day he was in his study when a man he knew from the neighborhood knocked on the door and said, "Father, do you want to buy a color TV?" It was back when color TVs were an exotic commodity. Charles asked, "What do you mean?" "We just got a shipment in from Nashville. Get you a good deal," the man said. "No thanks," Charles said, thinking to himself that the TVs must be hot, and there was no way he would buy one. He sat in his study for a few minutes, feeling a little inflated over his incredible insight into the obvious. Later that afternoon, the same man was involved in an armed robbery, during which a policeman was killed. Charles then thought to himself, "Maybe if I had bought a color TV, this man would have used the money to go off and get drunk or whatever, and I might have prevented this terrible tragedy…"

Charles lived with these feelings of guilt and doubt for years, until one day, as he was driving the streets of Louisville, he saw the very man who had tried to sell him the color TV, standing on a street corner in a suit and tie. Charles pulled over and offered the man a ride. The man told Charles he had been paroled from Eddyville, the state prison, and was working in a government program at the mayor's office. He said he had been involved in that terrible shooting, although he hadn't pulled the trigger, and said he felt genuine remorse.

Charles felt good about reconciling with this man, so he gathered some courage and said, "Do you remember years ago, the day of that terrible robbery, that you came by my study and wanted me to buy one of those color TVs?" The man said, "Yeah, I remember that." Charles said, "Did you really think I was that dumb? Surely you knew that I knew the TVs were hot." The man replied, "Father, you're dumber than I thought. There weren't any TVs."

And that's what we've been told all our lives. There are no color TVs, yet we've lived with feelings of doubt and guilt for so many of these years, thinking that there is a cause-and-effect cosmic order and that we have somehow contributed to evil through our mistakes, bad judgments, and moral failings. There are no color TVs or barns. They are illusions. They've tricked us and told us lies. Those barns have been built out of fear, and if those barns are going to be burned down, then love is the only flint that can make the spark, that creates the fire, that eliminates the fear.

These boxes, these barns we live behind—they're illusions. They never were there. They were built by consensus reality, and the collective mind-set, which desires adaptation and conformity, because things run more smoothly and there's less anxiety. When there is pluralism, when there are varieties of choices, then we begin to have problems, because anxieties, ambiguities, and ambivalences get created. If we homogenize and make everything mono-chromatic, then we don't have so much confusion, so much complexity, and therefore so much anxiety. We palliate and soothe it all with conformity and adaptation. Agape is the "hard and enduring" love that Flannery O'Connor wrote about, the love that is willing to risk anxiety, misunderstanding, lone-liness, and rejection because the love for another—or even oneself—is so great. To quote John I, "God is love, and those who dwell in love dwell in God, and God in them."

## BODY

The poet Eduardo Galliano writes that the church says the body is a sin, science says the body is a machine, advertising says the body is a business, but the body says, "I'm a fiesta." (Which is how we say "party" here in Texas.)[5]

That wild-eyed English engraver William Blake, who came outside of the barn to see the infinite, timeless nature of reality, offers a viewpoint that can help us open the door to a higher level of perception:

To see a World in a Grain of Sand
And a Heaven in a Wild Flower,
Hold Infinity in the palm of your hand
And Eternity in an hour.

Blake also reminds us that the five senses are the inlets to the soul. Vision, hearing, touch, smell, and taste—how could we celebrate life, love, and God without them? Regarding the latter, Bill Moyers was interviewing James Dickey, the great Southern poet, when he asked, "James, what's better about the South?" And Dickey replied, "Now, Billy, ain't you ever eat okrey?" (That's how some of us pronounce that sensual, heat-loving seedpod down here in the South.)

When Christ tells us through the act of the Eucharist, "This is my body, take and eat it," how can a Christian ever deny the body? The very idea that we would devalue the body when it provides the inlets to the soul and carries the redolent presence of the transcendent. The very idea that we would treat this gift of human sexuality as if it were dirty! I like that joke story about a man who asks his friend, "Do you think sex is dirty?" And the friend replies, "Yeah, if it's done right." Or as one of my analysts used to say, "Life's a mess, that's just the way it is—like good sex."

I've been a people helper for 30 years, and I've never had anybody come into my office without a body. The body seems to be important. It at least locates and identifies soul, but it is also the receptor for the soul to experi-ence the transcendent. Our bodies provide the most convenient and available way for us to encounter the source, but our ingrained patriarchal attitudes make us afraid of nature, instinct, and sensuality—all feminine qualities that everyone possesses, regardless of gender. This Augustinian attitude has cut us off from our bodies and has led us to regard the body as our enemy. Eros and sensuality don't disappear when we deny them, but only come back as pornography and misogynistic and homophobic attitudes. We can't get rid of our bodies, so we seek to manipulate them through denial, addiction, eating disorders, and cosmetic surgeries. Yet there is never enough to satisfy, so we keep on torturing ourselves, when all the body wants is to be loved and embraced by the soul living within it.

People talk about having bodies. "I am my body," you hear people say. I don't have a body. I am body. I'm a psychosomatic being, psyche and soma, the integration of psyche and body. It's time that we owned our bodies, that we lived in our bodies and belonged our bodies. We must celebrate our bodies, for they are our soul embodied.

## SUFFERING

Suffering is another way in which we can experience the transcendent, but who would consciously choose to suffer? Truth be told, probably no one, but the reality is that suffering seems to choose us, rather than the other way around. It is up to us whether we open ourselves to encountering the transcendent in our inevitable suffering, or whether we deny the possibility through our rampant and tempting varieties of distraction, sanctioned medication (antidepressants and the like), or self-medication (drug addiction, alcoholism, etc.).

By suffering, I'm not talking about the kind of nonproductive physical pain or true psychological disorders such as chemically rooted depression. That kind of pain and suffering should be palliated with all due urgency. What we learn from physical pain, especially, we learn in 10 minutes. The kind of suffering I'm talking about is soul suffering, and it seems to be a requirement for the building of soul.

I love the King James Version of the New Testament, where Jesus is giving his Sermon on the Mount, and he says, "Suffer the little children that come unto me and forbid them not, for such is the Kingdom of Heaven." Then Jesus took the children up in his arms and laid his hands upon them, indicating that to "suffer the children" means to pick them up by their bottoms. So here we have it from an authority no other than Jesus, that to suffer means "to carry from below," just as the etymology tells us.

To suffer in the spiritual sense means to carry something until we know its meaning. It is helpful to develop a teleological viewpoint, teleology coming from the root *teleos*, which means "complete" or "whole." When something happens that causes us to suffer, a teleological viewpoint leads us to ask, "What is this leading to? What truth can I discern from this suffering?" Of every accident, illness, difficulty, mistake, trauma, or tragedy, we must ask, "What does this want from me? What is its meaning?"

Perfection is not possible, it should not even be a goal. But our imperfect lives are nonetheless perfect just as they are, and there will inevitably be all of the difficulties and other travails I described above. They are not optional, but guaranteed. We are not asked to avoid suffering, but to discern the meaning and find the transcendence that always accompanies suffering, like the proverbial silver lining. This is available to us if we change our minds about suffering and see it as a natural process of soul making.

## DREAMS

Dreams are a convenient, natural way to experience *vox deo*, the voice of God or the Self. Like God, dreams come to us unbidden, but it is our duty to welcome and honor them. Conversely, we ignore their messages at our own peril, for the Self will do whatever it takes get our attention, including hitting us with the psychic equivalent of a sledgehammer.

Of all the spiritual practices that are important to me—and I consciously embrace every practice on this list—paying attention to my dreams carries the most meaning and profundity for me. It's a doorway to the transcendent that is open to every living soul. You don't have to be a Jungian analyst to analyze your dreams. In fact, only the dreamer can analyze her dreams, and they are chock full of information if we would just pay attention.

All you have to do is honor the dream. Write it and share it. Find a safe person, a beloved, teacher, analyst, or anybody that you trust to tell the dream. Telling the dream completes it. I learned about this at a very early age as a young priest in a poor urban neighborhood of Kansas City. I had been ordained so recently I could still smell the freshness of my black shirt. I was in my office one day when the church secretary called and said, "There's a lady here who wants to see the priest, and you're the only one in the building." You could tell her confidence in me! The visitor was a rough-looking woman from South America who could barely speak English, but somehow she had found her way to Kansas City and my church, perhaps through the hand of God to offer me a lesson. She called me *sacerdote*, Spanish for priest. She'd had a big dream, she said, and she came to give it to the *sacerdote*. We sat down, she told me the dream in her halting English, then just as quickly she got up, nodded to acknowledge me, and left.

I learned a lot that day. She was honoring the dream by taking it to a holy man. If you have a dream, pay attention, because in it there is information about you and your world. It's the voice of God, coming from the unconscious, if we believe in the *imago dei*, the image of God, that is in each of us. Jungians call it the Self, and the Self is the dream maker.

If we pay attention to our dreams over a lifetime, we will begin to see that the dreams have as much reality and are as much a part of our lives as the senior prom or our first marriage. The dream is the nightly appearance of the Self, with a whole mystical language that is ours to discover if (it bears repeating) only we have the eyes to see and the ears to hear.

There are many ways to experience the transcendent, if we believe that the transcendent is available to us in our daily pedestrian lives. Nature is available to us anytime, anywhere. Art and creativity are callings that we must express. Ritual process is that conscious putting of oneself in the context for the revelation of the transcendent, and a way of seeing that even our personal rituals can be sacred, sacramental moments. As for love, God is love—the rest is commentary. Our bodies are the embodiment of God. Suffering is not an appreciated or a pleasurable way to encounter the transcendent, but it is an important way, and it is with us regardless, so we might as well reap its rewards. And finally, God is our dreams every night.

Something big is going on in this world, bigger than we can comprehend. We don't know what it is, and we don't really have the consciousness to perceive it anyway, but let us consciously commit to believing that we are part of something bigger than ourselves, something to which we're willing to give ourselves, through which we'll discover ourselves. Even though we haven't a clue about this eternal circle, the center and circumference of which is everywhere.

I love the story Kurt Vonnegut told about two particles of yeast who sat around discussing the meaning of life and the universe, not realizing that at that very moment, they were making champagne. What is it we're about? Something big that we don't have a clue about, but it's going on and it's about time that we human beings opened ourselves to the experience of God, in the mundane and the ordinary, for that's where we will find the miraculous and the extraordinary. How do we get there? My strong admonition to you is to dismantle the structures, evict the infantilizing authorities, and burn down the goddamn barn.

# NOTES

## SERIES FOREWORD

1. L. Aden and J. H. Ellens, *Turning Points in Pastoral Care, The Legacy of Anton Boisen and Seward Hiltner* (Grand Rapids, MI: Baker, 1990). Anton Boisen was at the University of Chicago for decades and developed models for understanding the relationship between psychology and religion as well as between mental illness, particularly psychoses, and the forms of meaningful spiritual or religious experience. Seward Hiltner was one of a large number of students of Boisen who carried his work forward by developing theological and psychotherapeutic structures and modes that gave operational application to Boisen's ideas. Hiltner was on the faculty of Princeton Theological Seminary, in the chair of Pastoral Theology and Pastoral Psychology for most of his illustrious career. While Boisen wrote relatively little, Hiltner published profusely, and his works became notable contributions to church and society.

## PREFACE

1. C. G. Jung, Aion, *Researches into the Phenomenology of the Self (Collected Works of C. G. Jung Vol. 9 Part 2)* (Princeton: Princeton University Press, 1959), p. 93.

## CHAPTER 1

1. Karen Armstrong, *A Short History of Myth* (New York: Canongate, 2005), p. 122.
2. Ibid., p. 123.
3. Jane Jacobs, *Dark Age Ahead* (New York: Random House 2004), p. 55.
4. Robert Johnson, *Owning Your Own Shadow* (New York: HarperCollins, 1991), p. vii–viii.

## CHAPTER 2

1. Sam Harris, *Letter to a Christian Nation* (New York: Vintage Books, 2006), p. 80.
2. Jimmy Carter, *Our Endangered Values* (New York: Simon & Schuster, 2005), p. 32.

3. James Hollis, *Finding Meaning in the Second Half of Life* (New York: Gotham Books, 2005), pp. 164–65.

4. Ronald Kessler, "Facing your Fear." October 1, 2000. USA Weekend.com.

5. Interview on National Public Radio, "Fresh Air," May 8, 2006.

## CHAPTER 3

1. Robert Johnson, *Owning Your Own Shadow* (New York: Harper San Francisco, 1991), p. 5.

## CHAPTER 5

1. John Shelby Spong, *Why Christianity Must Change or Die* (New York: Harper-SanFrancisco, 1998), p. 143.

2. John P. Dourley, *The Illness That We Are: A Jungian Critique of Christianity* (Toronto: Inner City Books, 1984), p. 75.

3. Charles Kimball, *When Religion Becomes Evil* (New York: HarperCollins, 2002), p. 191.

4. *Synchronicity* was defined by Jung as an "acausal connecting principle."

5. C. G. Jung, *The Collected Works, Vol. 11* (Princeton: Princeton University Press, 1953–1979), p. 245.

## CHAPTER 6

1. James Hollis, *Mythologems* (Toronto: Inner City Books, 2004), p. 8.

2. John A. Buehrens and F. Forrester Church, *Our Chosen Faith* (Boston: Beacon Press, 1989), p. 93.

3. John A. Buehrens and F. Forrester Church, *Our Chosen Faith* (Boston: Beacon Press, 1989), p. 137–38.

## CHAPTER 7

1. Edward Edinger, *Ego and Archetype* (Boston: Shambhala Publications, 1972), p. 112.

2. Elaine Pagels, *The Gnostic Gospels* (New York: Vintage Books, 1989), p. 128.

3. Thich Nhat Hanh, *Calming the Fearful Mind* (Berkeley: Parallax Press, 2005), p. 88.

4. John A. Buehrens and F. Forrester Church, *Our Chosen Faith* (Boston: Beacon Press, 1989), p. 82.

5. John A. Sanford, *The Kingdom Within: The Inner Meaning of Jesus' Sayings* (New York: HarperCollins, 1987), p. 56.

6. Thomas Cahill, *How the Irish Saved Civilization* (New York: Nan A. Talese/Doubleday, 1995), p. 123.

7. Robert Johnson, *Femininity Lost and Regained* (New York: HarperCollins, 1991), p. 32.

## CHAPTER 8

1. John A. Sanford, *The Kingdom Within: The Inner Meaning of Jesus' Sayings* (New York: HarperCollins, 1987), p. 68.

2. Elaine Pagels, *The Gnostic Gospels* (New York: Vintage Books, 1989), p. 126.

3. Ibid., p. xv.

4. Ibid., p. 127.

## CHAPTER 9

1. Joseph Dispenza, *God on Your Own: Finding a Spiritual Path outside Religion* (San Francisco: Jossey-Bass, 2006), p. 86.

2. John P. Dourley, *The Psyche as Sacrament: A Comparative Study of C. G. Jung and Paul Tillich* (Toronto: Inner City Books, 1981), p. 38.

3. Thomas Cahill, *How the Irish Saved Civilization* (New York: Anchor Books, 1995), p. 116.

4. Robert Johnson, *Femininity Lost and Regained* (New York: HarperCollins, 1991), p. 26–27.

5. Frederic Brussat and Mary Ann Brussat, *Spiritual Literacy: Reading the Sacred in Everyday Life* (New York: Scribner, 1998), p. 369.

# Selected Bibliography

Armstrong, Karen. *A Short History of Myth*. New York: Canongate, 2005.

Cahill, Thomas. *How the Irish Saved Civilization*. New York: Nan A. Talese/Doubleday, 1995.

Carter, Jimmy. *Our Endangered Values: America's Moral Crisis*. New York: Simon & Schuster, 2005.

Dourley, John P. *The Illness That We Are: A Jungian Critique of Christianity*. Toronto: Inner City Books, 1984.

Hanh, Thich Nhat. *Calming the Fearful Mind: A Zen Response to Terrorism*. Berkeley: Parallax Press, 2005.

Harris, Sam. *Letter to a Christian Nation*. New York: Vintage Books, 2006.

Hollis, James. *Finding Meaning in the Second Half of Life*. New York: Gotham Books, 2005.

Hollis, James. *Mythologems*. Toronto: Inner City Books, 2004.

Johnson, Robert. *Femininity Lost and Regained*. New York: HarperCollins, 1991.

Johnson, Robert. *Owning Your Own Shadow*. New York: HarperCollins, 1991.

Jung, C. G. *The Collected Works, Vol. VII*. Princeton: Princeton University Press, 1953–1979.

Kimball, Charles. *When Religion Becomes Evil: Five Warning Signs*. New York: HarperCollins, 2002.

Pagels, Elaine. *The Gnostic Gospels*. New York: Vintage Books, 1989.

Sanford, John A. *The Kingdom Within: The Inner Meaning of Jesus' Sayings*. New York: HarperCollins, 1987.

Spong, John Shelby. *Jesus for the Non-Religious*. New York: HarperCollins, 2007.

# INDEX

## About the Authors

J. PITTMAN McGEHEE is a private-practice analyst. He teaches at University of Houston and is the director of The Institute for the Advancement of Psychology and Spirituality. He served, for 11 years, as Dean of Christ Church cathedral in Houston. He has held many distinguished lectureships, including the 1987 Harvey Lecture at the Episcopal Seminary of the Southwest in Austin; the 1988 Perkins Lecture in Wichita Falls; the 1990 Woodhull Lectures in Dayton; and the 1991 St. Luke's Lectures in Birmingham. He was the 1994 Rockwell Visiting Theologian at the University of Houston and 1996 Carolyn Fay Lecturer in Analytical Psychology also at the University of Houston.

DAMON J. THOMAS is a writer and editor living in Houston, Texas. He is the co-author of *Speaking from the Heart: Transforming Stage Fright and Telling Your Own Story* (co-written with Sandra Zimmer). An experienced journalist and public relations executive, Thomas has published numerous newspaper and magazine articles.

## About the Series Editor

J. HAROLD ELLENS is a research scholar at the University of Michigan, Department of Near Eastern Studies. He is a retired Presbyterian theologian and ordained minister, a retired U.S. Army colonel, and a retired professor of philosophy, theology, and psychology. He has authored, coauthored, or edited 165 books and 167 professional journal articles. He served 15 years as executive director of the Christian Association for Psychological Studies and as founding editor and editor-in-chief of the *Journal of Psychology and Christianity*. He holds a PhD from Wayne State University in the psychology of human communication, a PhD from the University of Michigan in biblical and Near Eastern studies, and master's degrees from Calvin Theological Seminary, Princeton Theological Seminary, and the University of Michigan. He was born in Michigan, grew up in a Dutch-German immigrant community, and determined at age seven to enter the Christian ministry as a means to help his people with the great amount of suffering he perceived all around him. His life's work has focused on the interface of psychology and religion.